Dismantling the Big Lie

The Protocols of the Elders of Zion

Dismantling the Big Lie

The Protocols of the
Elders of Zion

by

Steven Leonard Jacobs

and

Mark Weitzman

Preface by
Rabbi Abraham Cooper

Simon Wiesenthal Center
Los Angeles, Ca.

in association with
KTAV Publishing House, Inc.
Jersey City, N.J.

Library of Congress Cataloging-in-Publication Data

Jacobs, Steven L.
    Dismantling the big lie : the Protocols of the elders of Zion / by
Steven L. Jacobs and Mark Weitzman.
      p.   cm.
    Includes bibliographical references.
    ISBN 0-88125-785-0 (pbk.)—ISBN 0-88125-786-9 (hardcover)
    1. Protocols of the wise men of Zion.   2. Antisemitism.
I. Weitzman,
Mark. II. Title.
DS145.P7J33   2003
305.892'4—dc21

                                                2003014497

Published by
KTAV Publishing House, Inc.
930 Newark Avenue
Jersey City, NJ 07306
Email: *info@ktav.com*
www.ktav.com
(201) 963-9524
Fax (201) 963-0102

*For
Elisabeth Maxwell,
whose vision
has borne
fruit*

Table of Contents

Acknowledgments

———❦———

Grateful thanks and heartfelt appreciation are hereby expressed to all those without whom this project would never have seen the light of day: to Rabbis Marvin Hier and Abraham Cooper and the library of the Simon Wiesenthal Center, Los Angeles, for their encouragement, support, and funding; to Dorothy Margraf of Monee, Illinois, indefatigable Internet researcher and committed Jew, who continuously plied the author with invaluable source material; to the membership of Temple B'nai Sholom of Huntsville, Alabama, who supported the author during the initial writing and researching of the refutations, and who understood the significance of this undertaking and the need for it; to Dr. Elisabeth Maxwell of London, England, who first approached the authors after hearing Steven Jacobs' presentation on combating Holocaust denial, and who believed that the two of us should attempt this work—her vision framed the entire project, and therefore, it is to her that it is dedicated; and finally, to my wife Louanne and son Shea, who remain my sources of inspiration and joy.

Steven Leonard Jacobs

While there are many people who have contributed in various ways to this book, there are some whose contributions have been so great that they deserve special acknowledgement. Rabbi Marvin Hier's leadership and inspiration created the institutional framework for this project. Rabbi Abraham Cooper read the manuscript at every stage of its development, and provided suggestions and encouragement on an almost daily basis. This work would never have been completed without his efforts. My colleagues Rick Eaton, Abbee Corb, Shimon Samuels, Adaire Klein, Nancy Saul, Marcial Lavina, Elisa Vandernoot and Lauren Hellman have all been extraordinarily helpful in providing the benefits of their expertise. Special thanks to Jamie Hoffer for the jacket design. I am also grateful to my colleagues in New York, Rhonda Barad, Sydney Pringle and to my assistant, Dion Duyck (and to Elana Silver who preceded her) for their support, patience and constant good humor. Simon Wiesenthal has been both an inspiration and mentor to me as to so many others; being able to share his friendship has been an even greater privilege.

Professors Fred Schweitzer and Charles Raffel read the manuscript and their comments and suggestions saved the text from many errors and were extremely helpful.

Rabbi Yitzhak Etshalom reviewed the entire text and contributed many suggestions regarding classical Jewish sources. In essence, he also functioned as a co-author of the book.

Bernie Scharfstein and Adam Bengal have welcomed this project with opened arms, and shaped it into a presentable form. We are grateful for their efforts

Finally, this work could never have been completed without the patience and encouragement of those closest to me: my father Harry, of blessed memory, and my mother Leah, who both taught me by word and example, my wife Elaine, whose love constantly alters my life for the better, and my sons Yaron and Ilan, who provide me with daily doses of joy, pride and hope.

Mark Weitzman

Preface

The Bible teaches: *m'dvar sheker tirchak*—"distance yourself from falsehood" (Leviticus 19:1), but what to do when falsehood stalks you? From time immemorial, the Jewish people have been victimized by one "big lie" after another. In the fourteenth century, the Jews were blamed for the Black Plague, which claimed 25 million victims in the span of five short years. From the Middle Ages into the twenty-first century, Jews have stood accused of ritually murdering gentile children for use in their Passover matzah, and according to mainstream Saudi media sources, even in their Purim pastries (hamantaschen). A half-century after Auschwitz, the victims are mocked, their martyrdom and suffering denied, as professional Holocaust "revisionists" pedal their agenda of antisemitism and hate.

But of all the anti-Jewish screeds, it is the *Protocols of the Elders of Zion* that emboldens and empowers antisemites. While other antisemitic works may have a sharper intellectual base, it is the conspiratorial imagery of the *Protocols* that has fueled the imagination and hatred of Jews and Judaism, from captains of industry like Henry Ford, to teenage Hamas homicide bombers.

The geographic reach of the *Protocols* is astounding. On my first visit to Japan in 1985, the book was on sale at the Tokyo Hilton, right next to another perpetual bestseller, *The Diary of Anne Frank*! And at least one Japanese author, Masami Uno, wrote a *Protocols* rip-off that sold millions of copies, ascribing every one of society's social and economic ills to the Jews—a people virtually unknown in a nation that boasted a Jewish population of 1,500 out of a total of 130,000,000 citizens! But as was explained to me by my Japanese friends, "It's nothing personal, rabbi. Most of us have never met a Jew, but many of us are seeking a simple explanation for the increasingly complex challenges thrown our way."

This profound need also explains why the *Protocols*, a product of tsarist Christian Russia, has been wholeheartedly embraced in the Arab and Muslim world. The peoples of the Middle East, a region awash in the riches of oil but devoid of democratic opportunity, seek explanations for their failure to achieve economic parity with the rest of the world and especially their inability to contain the open, democratic Jewish state in their midst. The *Protocols* offers "expert" confirmation in the Arab world for the widely held view of Jews as conniving, amoral, power-hungry conspirators.

As a result, the *Protocols* are deployed in many social and political contexts. For example, basing the 48-part miniseries *Horseman Without a Horse* on the *Protocols* guaranteed huge ratings for its Egyptian TV prime-time airing during the Muslim holy month of Ramadan.

The *Protocols* are widely available in the Palestinian Authority. When it was proposed that the PLO Charter be formally amended to drop its call for the destruction of Israel, Rafat Najar, an official of the Palestinian Council, parried the suggestion with a demand that "in exchange for changing the charter . . . [there should be] a change in the Protocols of Zion"!

In September 2001, just days before the horrific events of 9/11, I and other Jewish delegates were trapped in a stadium in Durban, South Africa at the United Nations World Conference on Racism, as 17,000 Muslims protested against Israel outside. Some carried banners reading "Hitler should have finished the job," and the organizers peddled copies of the *Protocols* to passersby.

From Black Muslim stands on the streets of Manhattan, to the bookstalls in Buenos Aires, Madrid, Athens to publishing houses in Prague and Kuwait City, the *Protocols* and the infection of mistrust, fear, ignorance, and hate spreads.

Not even Tancred Golenpolsky's historic 1993 victory in a Moscow courtroom succeeded in erasing the allure of the *Protocols*. A lawsuit brought by the xenophobic Pamyat group asserted that the *Protocols* was a legitimate historical work. I attended part of those proceedings and am proud that the Wiesenthal Center helped defend the beleaguered Jewish publisher, but not even a Russian judge's pronouncement, in the very land where the *Protocols* had been concocted, that the book was in fact an antisemitic forgery has succeeded in denting its popularity.

So why now? There are already masterful works by scholars like Norman Cohn and Hadassah Ben-Itto that explore the *Protocols* in great depth. Why publish another detailed response to this "big lie"?

There are three reasons:

First, this is the only work to refute the *Protocols* item by item. This systematic approach is the first line of defense against the current wholesale embracing and promotion of the pernicious imagery of the *Protocols* by government-controlled media in the Middle East—from state-sanctioned TV miniseries to the charter of the Hamas organization—to legitimize terrorism against Jews. Meanwhile, in the supposedly enlightened Western democracies, the senior Laborite parliamentarian in the United Kingdom insists that a Jewish cabal manipulated Prime Minister Blair into participating in the war in Iraq, even as American conservative commentator Pat Buchanan charged that Jewish neoconservatives were the chief architects and cheerleaders for the U.S.-led war. This important book enables non-Jewish readers to recognize the distortions of the *Protocols* and see what Jewish teachings and traditions really say about the questions they raise. The Jewish reader now has a resource to rebut these pernicious lies whenever and wherever encountered.

Second is the Internet, where conspiracy theories of all stripes are cloaked in legitimacy within the virtual walls of attractive Web sites. Millions of young, impressionable Internet users are easy prey for the ultimate "blame the Jews" scenario. The unprecedented exposure this debunked book is receiving online demands renewed attention and new efforts to counter its hate. This excellent work by Dr. Steven Leonard Jacobs and Mark Weitzman provides a clear refutation of every charge against the Jews and Judaism set down in the *Protocols*, so that the vanguard of our community, including students on campuses, can rebut every canard.

There is a third reason. The Talmud (Shabbat 104a) and the Zohar both assert that *sheker ain lo raglayim*, literally, "falsehood has no legs." The search for and commitment to truth is a foundation of the Jewish tradition and, as the *Ethics of the Fathers*, a tractate of the Mishnah, reminds us, is one of the three pillars of civilization. As Jews we fight falsehood because we must, as Americans living in the greatest democracy we fight falsehood because we can.

Finally, the *Protocols* presents every concerned citizen with another challenge. In 2000, following an ugly confrontation over the *Protocols*, I was invited to speak to a group of 150 Japanese writers and editors in Tokyo. After my two-hour presentation, my host raised his hand and asked:

"Dear rabbi, we now know that the *Protocols* is a fraud and that you Jews don't do these terrible things in your synagogues. but please, rabbi, tell us—what do Jews do in their synagogues?" This humbling query should remind us all that ultimately, our greatest enemy may not be bigotry, but ignorance.

Rabbi Abraham Cooper

Los Angeles
Passover, 2003

The following are examples of some of the editions and versions of the Protocols available worldwide.

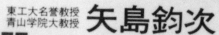

東工大名誉教授
青山学院大教授 矢島鈞次

これからの10年間
ユダヤ・プロトコール超裏読み術

あなたに起こる
ショッキングな現実

PLAYBOOKS

なぜ確かなのか―この恐るべき予言書

プロトコールの裏読みがつかんだ
この先10年のショッキングな現実を明かす

青春出版社

How to Read the Hidden Meaning in the Jewish Protocols: Revealing the Shocking Facts That Will Happen to You in the Next Decade. Japan, 1986.

СИОНСКИЕ ПРОТОКОЛЫ

Russia, 1992.

The image reflects a classic antisemitic stereotype. England, 1978.

The Invisible World Government, or the Jewish Program to Subjugate the World. Spain, 1930.

The Jewish Danger: Complete Text of the Protocols of the Elders of Zion. France, 1934.

Published during the Nazi occupation of Poland in 1943.

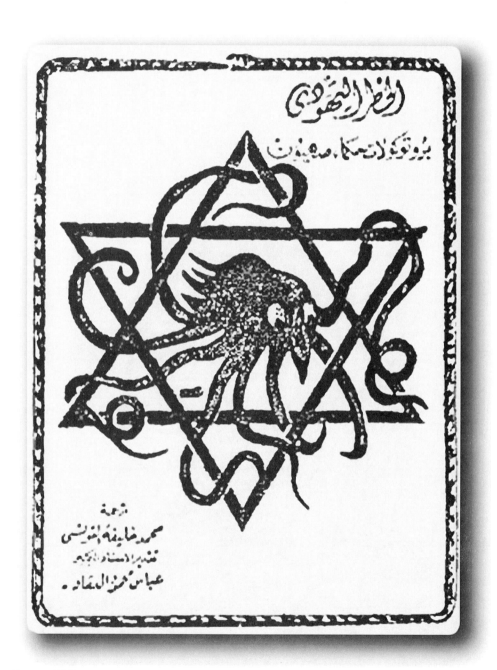

Egypt, 1972.

عجاج نويهض

بروتوكولات
حكماء صهيون

المجلد الثاني

الجزء الثالث والجزء الرابع

الطبعة الثانية مزيدة

Damascus, 1990.

The Protocols Today: Virtual and Real

The Protocols of the Learned Elders of Zion have often been discredited, and in the words of one contemporary writer "were written for the idiot,"[1] but a recent technological development has given the work new life and an unprecedented global reach. The growth of the Internet and the World Wide Web has mainstreamed hate and made all sorts of crackpot theories, canards, and unsubstantiated accusations available to millions of people around the world. And, out of all these theories, it is perhaps the message and imagery of the *Protocols* that have benefited the most.

By the spring of 2003 the Internet was available to an audience of approximately 620 million people. While originally most of these users were located in North America, the last few years have seen an explosion in international use that has further increased the global potential and importance of this medium for communication and education. Recent statistics show that of those 620 million users, only 40 percent were classified as using English as their main language, while Asian languages were now up to an online presence of 26 percent (http://glreach .com/globstats/indExodusphp).

Not surprisingly, as a result of this trend, various right-wing, Islamist and other extremists have embraced the digital world as a powerful way to spread their message across borders and to an ever-widening circle of readers. When we compare this new method of communication with older methods, such as

---

1. Stephen Eric Bronner, *A Rumor About the Jews*, p. 130.

letters, flyers, or handouts, we can see why extremists view e-culture as an unprecedented historic opportunity to penetrate the mainstream of society with their agenda.

The Internet offers another bonus for extremists. The online audience is often composed of teenagers and children. As is well known, the Internet appeals more to younger users than to the older generations. For many of these youth, the Internet has become their primary source of *all* information. What is available online, therefore, has an unprecedented influence in shaping their ideas and opinions and helping to shape the future of society.

The Internet has been hailed as a revolutionary environment where information can be posted by anybody for anybody. While enthusiasts of the new technology see this as a boon for the unfettered transmittal and exchange of information, we must acknowledge that there are problems that come along with this opportunity. For example the Internet has no librarian, editor, or fact-checker, and so information that is false or misleading can be presented in a visually attractive and convincing framework. In such an environment, the unsuspecting reader, especially the young reader, has no way of discerning the "big lie" from ultimate truth. The *Protocols* present, then, a classic pre-cyber conspiratorial plot, tailor-made for a revival in the digital age.

Another benefit for extremists who use the Internet is the ability to be anonymous. By not having to expose their true identities, they can promote their hateful agendas while evading both legal and social responsibility. Freed of any consequence of their online postings, the Internet also removes any inhibitions in promoting racism, antisemitism, violence, and even terrorism. While not all cases of hateful postings lead to action, these initiatives have inspired hate and violent crimes aimed at members of minorities or at disrupting society as a whole.

And, when antisemitism and conspiracy are linked together, it is often the *Protocols* that is the text used to justify and substantiate demonization and hatred of the Jew.

Not surprisingly, then, the *Protocols* appear online either in the complete version or as a source or proof for outrageous antisemitic charges. If we take the time to examine its online presence, we can learn much about the *Protocols* and their contemporary promoters.

Online booksellers are an important source for obtaining the *Protocols*. Online companies have made a policy of *not* making judgments about the material they sell. One of the more disturbing practices of this portion of the online economy is the use of book reviews written by readers to sell the titles. Reviewers with no credentials other than their own prejudices are presented to the online shopper as impartial voices urging purchase of the *Protocols* and other hate-filled books. This practice has gotten so out of hand that negative media attention and public protest have forced key online booksellers to revise the policy. Another e-commerce policy that helped project hate globally was the practice of selling the *Protocols* and other hate books by U.S.-based companies to customers in countries like France, Germany, and Canada. These transactions occurred despite the fact that these democracies had laws that forbade the importing and distribution of hate materials. Major U.S. online booksellers were confronted by European governments and activists and have begun to refuse to ship the *Protocols* where it is illegal.

The *Protocols* are not just sold online, they appear as a support or basis for many wild and malicious accusations and theories.

Perhaps most extreme are those who cite the *Protocols* as the blueprint for the terrorist attacks of September 11, 2001. For example, they explain the terrorist attacks of 9/11 as part of an unfolding plan. "In the wake of the terrorist attack on the World Trade Center, and the Pentagon, certain parties . . . are using the nation's heightened concern about security to advance a long standing agenda." This agenda is later made explicit when the site adds: "We are getting closer every day to the absolute dictatorship envisioned by the *Protocols of the Learned Elders of Zion*" (www.americanholocaust50megs.com/National_PoliceForce. htm). Another site, this time posted by an Islamist extremist, defines 9/11 in this manner: "The benumbing sudden cataclysm of September 11 was engineered by Mossad with the help of Israelis in America. A study of the Zionist *Protocols* and its related literature shows what has been happening in the contemporary world" (Tariq Majeed, "The Design for Provoking A Global Clash," www.verity.nu/reality/clash.htm).

We find the *Protocols* serving as a source for those who choose to use hate as an explanation of political events either in the U.S. ("Clinton is patterning his actions after the precepts of the Satanic document, the *Protocols*," www.cuttingedge.org/news/n1217b.cm) or internationally (Compuserb, quoting Protocol 7 at www.compuserb.com/proto7htmn). Those who use the *Protocols* for this purpose are often people who feel powerless, who feel that world events are spinning out of control. They create a figure whose activities explain why the world is not operating in the way they want. This figure is the Jew, who in the *Protocols* can be both communist and capitalist, both democrat and tyrant. Thus the Jew can be used to fit any stereotypical need, to explain any crisis or challenge to the reader's worldview.

Of course, when Jews are actually involved in political events, as in the Middle East, the *Protocols* become an even more potent tool. It has become a staple of online anti-Zionism, especially since the resurgence of Palestinian violence in the Holy Land in October/November 2000. One site (http://forislam.com/aqsa/jews/zion/msp.htm) describes the *Protocols* as the source of "The Zionist Dream," depicted on a map that shows an exaggerated "Greater Israel." (The map also links Jews and Freemasons.) Another site (www.globaldomination.org.uk/proto2.html) combines various elements. A Muslim site based in Britain alleges that the *Protocols* are *the* source for a Jewish plan to achieve "global domination."

The use of the *Protocols* is not limited to political agendas. Another prominent area that relies on the *Protocols* online is religiously-inspired hatred. This hate often appears when believers in one religion need to denigrate other beliefs in order to justify their own faith. Thus the claim that the *Protocols* are proof-positive that Judaism is evil. A classic example of this is an extremist Christian site which proclaims that the *Protocols* are "Babylonian in origin" and were denounced by Jesus (www.roytaylorministries.com/am00058m). This site also has a political slant.

Another "Christian" site contrasts "Jesus' doctrine" to the *Protocols*, thus showing the "grave dangers that the *Protocols* present to the Christian world" (www.endtimesprophecy.net/~tttbs/EPN-1/Articlescnsp/prot.004.htmlanchor844786). Meanwhile, the International Christian Educational Service claims that the *Protocols* present "a program for the enslavement of the world and the destruction of Christian Religion" (www.holy war.org/protocol/protocol.html). For these sites, the *Protocols*, by creating the illusion of a threat where none exists, serve to alert the "true believer" who sees the world moving away from his or her faith. Rather than confront the challenges of a changing world, such true believers find it easier to blame all changes and all evil on a dangerous conspiracy, no matter how ridiculous or absurd the so-called conspiracy may seem to anyone else.

Another manifestation of the conspiratorial mindset rests in the belief that the news media, which both report the news and shape public opinion, are a part of the Jewish conspiracy. In this view, the conspiracy controls the flow of information, and thus manipulates and controls public opinion. Believers in the conspiracy often rely on the *Protocols* as a core document for this idea. One such believer uses music to express the idea, recording a song and posting the lyrics on his Web site. The song is called "The News Behind the News" and has as its chorus the lyrics:*

It's the news behind the news and the methods you can use,
   It's the blueprint and the plan they all rely on
   And it's within the *Protocols of the Learned Elders of Zion*.

The *Protocols*, ironically enough, have taken on a new identity on some Internet sites as an icon of free speech. On these sites (a quick search on a major search engine, Google, using the key words "*Protocols of Elders of Zion*" and "censorship" turned up 45 pages with a total of almost 450 hits), the fact that the *Protocols* have been discredited, and therefore dropped by reputable libraries and booksellers, is described as an example of censorship. Readers are urged to embrace the *Protocols* in the name of free speech. Some of these sites include disclaimers that they abhor and reject the content of the *Protocols*, but others find free speech a convenient excuse to not only endorse the *Protocols*, but to try to attract others to this "forbidden fruit." An example of

*Carl Klang, "The News Behind the News" http:www.klang.com/thenews.html.

the first category is a site that opposes censorship from a woman's perspective, and uses the *Protocols* as an example of "images that offend us" yet that still should be available to all (www .io..com/~wwwomen/aboutc). An example of the second category is the site that introduces links to the *Protocols* (and other racist and antisemitic sites) with the assertion that these links are presented "despite the best efforts . . . to censor 'objectionable' ideas" (www.stormfront.com).

While most of the Web sites mentioned above are in English, the Internet has become increasingly international in scope. As a result, for example, one site carries the *Protocols* online in English, French, German, Italian, Portuguese, Russian, Spanish, Swedish, Danish, Hungarian, and Arabic (www.abbc3.com). Another site now brings them to us in Serbian. A South African site that billed itself as the "*Protocols* Research Institute" (now offline) presented itself as a scholarly and objective look at the *Protocols*. This Internet presentation actually portrayed the book as an objective historical truth, containing facts vital for today's world. To further support this position, the Web site unveiled a "New *Protocols*" designed to update the tired and outdated references in the original. These "New *Protocols*" were written by Dr. William Pierce, who, before his death in July 2002, was one of the world's leading neo-Nazis. Pierce also authored *The Turner Diaries*, a book that served as a blueprint for Timothy McVeigh's bombing of the Federal Building in Oklahoma City in 1995, the worst case of domestic terrorism in U.S. history.

At the time of writing this book, a search on the Google search engine for "the *Protocols of the Elders of Zion*" turned up 11,100 hits. The complete text of the *Protocols* can be found on approximately 100 different sites. For a text that has so often been discredited, it is staggering to find such a resonance in the digital world. Barely 60 years since the end of World War II and the Nazi Holocaust, one of the major influences on Adolf Hitler is back in worldwide circulation.

And, via the Internet, it can be found on sites that use it to promote prejudice and hate. Even more important, these sites present the *Protocols*, not as discredited nonsense, but as a factual work providing real insights into how today's world really functions. Further, since the World Wide Web makes no allowances for an editorial or critical function, a Web site sponsor can present fiction as fact and fantasy as reality, replete with links to other, similarly-minded digital addresses. In such an environment, the truth and the Internet visitor can be overwhelmed by a sophisticated digital agenda of lies and prejudice.

It remains our collective responsibility to teach our children to approach *any* data on the Internet with a healthy dose of critical thinking. All the more with regard to fabrications like the *Protocols* must we prepare students and readers to be able to recognize the truth and to sort out history from fantasy.

When all this has been done, the *Protocols* will be exposed to new generations for what they really are: a tissue of outdated fantasy and lies, resurrected in the twenty-first-century virtual world of the Internet to inspire an antisemitism and hatred that is all too real and deadly.

IMPACT OF THE PROTOCOLS

The *Protocols* have already, unfortunately, had an enormous influence on the world. As one of the major influences on Adolf Hitler, they contributed greatly to making the twentieth century known as the century of genocide. Yet, while Hitler died in 1945, Hitlerism did not, and, although Nazism has been discredited in the view of most of the world, antisemitism lives on both as private philosophy and public policy.

The *Protocols* have become a Bible of anti-Zionism, adopted by enemies of the State of Israel to justify their attempts to destroy it. Thirty years ago the king of Saudi Arabia distributed copies of the *Protocols* to foreign guests. Eight years ago they were cited as authoritative by leaders of HAMAS and other Muslim extremists, who claimed, "Their [i.e. Zionists] scheme has been laid out in the Protocols."[2] Today, the *Protocols* continue to serve the same purpose, used by governments, organizations, and individuals to whip up hate against Israel and Jews. For example, Palestinian sources claim that Israeli policy is guided by the *Protocols*, and that the text also explains how Zionists control the United States.[3] In 2000 the Iranian government published a new edition of the *Protocols*, with an introduction that linked the classic text of antisemitism to the current attempt to destroy Israel. That was followed by the appearance of a series of articles based on the *Protocols* in *Al-Ahram*, Egypt's leading newspaper. The series answered the question "What exactly do the Jews want?' with the reply "Read what the Ninth Protocol of the *Protocols of the Elders of Zion* says."[4] In 2001, the *Protocols* were distributed by the Palestine Solidarity Committee of South Africa at the failed World Conference Against Racism in Durban, South Africa. Both Egyptian and Palestinian TV ran a thirty-part series that was based, according to an Egyptian weekly, on the idea

2. HAMAS charter, Article 32, translated by R. Israeli, and also available online at http://www.palestinecenter.org/cpap/documents/charter.html. First English translation published by Simon Wiesenthal Center, 1988.

3. Itamar Marcus, *In Their Own Words: Antisemitism and Racism as Policy in the Palestinian Authority*, pp. 17–18.

4. *Al-Ahram* (Egypt), June 23, 2001, cited in MEMRI (Middle East Media Research Institute) Special Dispatch—Egypt, July 9, 2001, No. 238.

that the *Protocols* are "the central line that still, to this very day, dominates Israel's policy, political aspirations and racism." According to the creator of the series, nineteen of the twenty-four protocols have already been implemented, and so "we must expect that the rest also will."[5] The *Protocols* have even been sighted recently in the gift shops of five-star hotels "from Jordan to Iran"![6]

But it is not only in the Middle East that the *Protocols* are once again prominent. In Europe, a Czech publisher recently republished the book, as also happened in Hungary (the Czech government prosecuted the publisher, while in Hungary, Protestant and Catholic groups condemned the publication of the book). In Russia, the original source of the *Protocols*, the text is still venerated in certain circles. In January 2001, outside of Moscow, a conference was held by members of the Orthodox church honoring the memory of Sergei Nilus, the original publisher of the *Protocols*, and they denounced the triple threat of the "tripartite serpent"—"Judaism, Papism, and Freemasonry." The *Protocols* are currently circulating not only in Europe, but in South America and Australia, and even in Japan.

Wherever they have appeared, the *Protocols* have served as a pretext for hate. Today, their function is extremely important for validating antisemitism. With the pseudo-scientific antisemitism of Nazi Germany totally discredited, those who are searching for a justification for their hatred of Jews have had to look elsewhere. And, with the rejection of religious antisemitism by all mainstream branches of Christianity, the conspiracy theory propounded in the *Protocols* is all that is left. But, while other forms of antisemitism have been discredited, the *Protocols* tap into what one historian calls "the most pernicious anti-Jewish imagery [which] involves stereotypes alleging mortal threats purportedly posed by Jews."[7]

5. *Roz AL-Youssuf* (Egypt), November 17, 2001, cited in MEMRI (Middle Eastern Media Research Institute) Special Dispatch—Arab Antisemitism, no. 309, Dec. 6, 2001.

6. Frank Rich, *New York Times*, "The Booing of Wolfowitz," May 11, 2002, online.

7. Robert Chazan. *Medieval Stereotypes and Modern Antisemitism*, Berkeley: University of California Press, 1996.

The claim that the leaders of world Jewry have for centuries been plotting to control the world not only excuses antisemitism, but makes it a virtue. By opposing the Jews, antisemites who believe this turn themselves into heroes fighting to liberate society. For the anti-Zionist, the *Protocols* justify efforts to destroy the State of Israel, which is viewed as a key element in the Jewish plot. Having imported the *Protocols* from the West, Muslim antisemitism has brought them back into the play of international affairs.

One of the most difficult decisions we faced with this book was whether to reprint the original text of the *Protocols* to accompany our refutation, or whether to just rely on summaries and paraphrases of the *Protocols* to keep the reader connected to the original text. After much consideration, and although it might seem odd that in a book devoted to refuting and rendering the *Protocols* as harmless as possible, we ultimately decided to reprint the original text in its entirety. Our choice was based on our belief that allowing the readers of this refutation to see the original text for themselves outweighed the drawback of distributing yet another copy of the *Protocols*. This decision was not made lightly: but when we considered that the *Protocols* are now available in a variety of languages to anyone who has access to the Internet, and, in certain parts of the world, particularly the Middle East, are distributed in mass media and with government support, it was apparent that access to the *Protocols* had become available to the widest audience ever in the inglorious history of this text. We also felt that having the original text of the *Protocols* available allows the reader to be certain that what we claim is written in the *Protocols* is, in fact, accurate. In other words, by reprinting the *Protocols*, the reader can see that the *Protocols* do indeed make these evil claims about Jews and Judaism, and that our book does not exaggerate or make up these accusations in our refutation of each specific protocol. In this approach we are following one of the earliest fighters against the *Protocols*, Cyrus Adler, who in a letter to Louis Marshall in 1919 wrote: "If this document [the *Protocols*] is being circulated extensively in any private way, my own first opinion would be that the best course to pursue would be to have it published and denounced for the fraud that it is,"[8] While it is a sad commentary that almost a century later this work is still necessary, it is our hope that this refutation will help restore the *Protocols* to the oblivion they so richly deserve.

The *Protocols* were written in a shroud of secrecy in an attempt to prop up the faltering government of imperial Russia. Their strange path has taken them throughout the world, where they have been used to support almost every imaginable conspiracy theory. Connecting to centuries-old antisemitic images and beliefs, the *Protocols* have been able to breathe new life into ancient hate. They have tapped into hidden fears and unspoken anxieties, giving some an explanation for a world in which they no longer feel in control. When events go in unexpected or unwanted directions, it is often easier for those who are frustrated by their inability to control the world to look for an explanation that removes self-responsibility and replaces it with a convenient target. Thus, despite all the historical, literary, and legal evidence that they are a forgery, the *Protocols* have persisted till this day. And, thus, the refutation in this volume, aimed not at the fanatical believer, but at the honest and critical reader, is still necessary today, more than a half a century after the Holocaust. For, ultimately, the *Protocols* are very similar to the classic myths of antiquity and the current delusions of the psychotic. They explain why a world that is desired does not exist, and root the fault not in our actions, but in a great conspiracy by evil Jews. Since only extreme measures can explain this global crisis, the *Protocols of the Learned Elders of Zion*, a text that is ridiculous to any sensible reader, but that can appear to be valid to the uninformed, real to the naive, and useful to the bigot, requires this refutation, lest the *Protocols* become, once again, as in the title of Norman Cohn's classic book, a "Warrant for Genocide."[9]

8. (*Cyrus Adler, Selected Letters vol. I.* Ira Robinson, ed. Philadelphia: JPS, 1985, pp. 402–403).

9. Cohn, Norman. *Warrant for Genocide: The Myth of the Jewish World Conspiracy and The Protocols of the Elders of Zion.* New York: Harper & Row, 1967.

Introduction and Rationale

Conspiracy Theory: Why Conspiracy?

Among the most problematic of human traits, history has consistently shown us, is our refusal to look ourselves directly in the mirror, admit that our failures are the result of our own doing, and begin the processes of correction and non-repetition. This fact of human existence holds not only for persons, but for nations. The most obvious modern historical example, relevant to this project, is Germany's defeat in the First World War due to superior adversaries and poor military and political decision-making. Adolf Hitler and his Nazi minions were able to gain power, at least partly, by convincing their defeated nation that the defeat was *not* of their own doing, but was the result of treason and betrayal by a subversive Fifth Column in league with their enemies, namely the Jews. In doing so, Hitler built upon the historic foundation of Jews as "outside the parameters of responsibility." Even more important, he drew upon the human weakness and propensity for conspiracy theory.

How much easier to blame others rather than ourselves for our failures! Especially when their religion differs from ours and is perceived as strangely exotic, when their political status as non-citizens makes them vulnerable as "guests" of the host society, and when all the ills of society can be attributed to their supposed power elevated to an almost mystical status by demagogic leaders. Add to this a forged and false document attesting to the out-group's evil plans and designs, and one has the psychological rationale that explains why disaffected human beings are so willing to accept conspiracy theories and why the fiction of *The Protocols of the Learned Elders of Zion* has endured for so long.

Why the Jews: The Cancer of Antisemitism

Simply defined, antisemitism is hatred of the Jewish people and the Jewish faith, heritage, and traditions. Evidence of it is first glimpsed in the Bible in the Pharaoh of Egypt's perception of his Israelite subpopulation as "the enemy" (Exodus, chap. 1), and is echoed by the prime minister of Persia in the Book of Esther. In both instances, the antisemitism is both politically and culturally motivated, with the vulnerable Jewish populations seen as outsiders. With the birth and spread of Christianity and the parting of the way between these two religious traditions, a further element is added: a religio-theological basis for antisemitism buttressed by a New Testament which holds the Jewish people primarily responsible for the death of the Christ, and sees the Romans, subtly manipulated by the Jews of Palestine, as only secondarily responsible.

Politics, culture, and religion were the three primary arrows in the quiver of the antisemites of Western civilization until the advent of Nazism, which emphasized a fourth, equally false and pernicious element: that of race or biology; understanding the religion of Judaism to have a *physical* basis and the people called Jews to be united by physically distinct characteristics (skin tone, hair color and texture, skull formation, nose and lip structure, etc.) different from those of the rest of the population. Equally, the Nazis made use of "genetic traits," supposedly honed over the centuries, which made European peoples vulnerable to the Jew: superior economic propensities, aggressive sexual proclivities, and "street smarts" rather than true intellectual ability.

Throughout the last two thousand years, antisemitism has not been confined to words alone, but has been coupled, at times, with the most dastardly of deeds. Despite periods of enlightenment and genuine and sincere friendship, Jews have been subjected to forced ghettoization, expulsion from countries of origin and residence, forced conversion, and extermination and annihilation.

Even this cursory survey of antisemitic thought and activity, which could be supplemented by specific historical examples from every country in Western Europe and the Americas, reveals the long-standing nature of antisemitism and its cancerous impact upon society. A people that has been historically, demographically, economically, politically, and militarily small has consistently found itself at the mercy of the larger population in its struggle to survive. But it has survived!

The Holocaust and the Birth of Israel

The years 1933–1945 would have realized the death of the entire European Jewish population had Hitler and those who allied themselves with him been successful. Almost 6 million men, women, and children, better than 50 percent of European Jewry, were wiped out in less that two decades. Yet, like the proverbial phoenix rising from the ashes, three years later, the Third Jewish Commonwealth, the State of Israel, was reborn on its ancient soil.

Both events have added to the antisemite's quiver. As the twenty-first century begins, so-called Holocaust deniers continue to parade their lies that the most documented of all genocides never occurred. They attribute to the State of Israel more political power than it possesses internationally, and depict those who support its right to exist and defend it among the community of nation-states as allies in some master cabal.

Add to all of this the nineteenth-century antisemitic forgery *The Protocols of the Learned Elders of Zion,* based on an earlier mid-nineteenth-century French political satire that had nothing whatsoever to do with Jews, and all the players are in place to sustain one of the greatest of antisemitic myths: that there exists a world Jewish conspiracy to take over, subjugate, and manipulate the peoples of the world for economic and other self-serving Jewish ends.

Uniqueness of Text Approach

The "story" of *The Protocols of the Learned Elders of Zion* is a relatively brief one. Much literature has already been generated to tell it, assess its impact, discuss its possible or probable authorship, and the like. Far less attention has been paid to the *content* of the document, its lies and accusations, not to mention its historical and religious inaccuracies. What is therefore unique in the present work is the deconstruction of this most famous of all antisemitic writings, protocol by protocol, revealing, perhaps for the first time, the utter absurdity of its accusations, the emptiness of its content, and the illogic of its arguments.

Those already convinced of the "truth" of the absurd claims presented by the *Protocols* will not be swayed. Nor will those who know what lies it contains. Readers who are coming to this document for the first time are invited to think critically for themselves, despite what they may have previously heard or read, and to draw their own conclusions.

In Brief: The Story of the Protocols

In 1864, a French lawyer, Maurice Joly, published a satire entitled *Dialogue aux Enfers entre Machiavel et Montesquieu, ou la politique aux xixe siècle* ("Conversation in Hell Between Machiavelli and Montesquieu, on the Politics of the Nineteenth Century") for which he was later to pay with his life. This satiric text of French politics made no reference whatsoever to Jews or Judaism, but did discuss the possibility that the masses were being politically manipulated for economic and other ends by superior persons.

It is believed that agents of the Russian secret service (the Okhrana) in France at the close of the nineteenth century, aware of the First Zionist Congress in Basel, Switzerland, which was chaired by Theodor Herzl, in August 1897, saw the political possibilities of this satire for use back home, although the identity of the person or persons who originally adapted it from the French to the Russian remains in doubt. The text they produced was published in Russia in 1903 by an Orthodox priest by the name of Sergei Nilus as an addendum to his own book, *The Great in the Small*. After the Russian Revolution of 1917, the text began to have a life of its own. Although it was exposed as a forgery by Philip Graves of *The Times* of London in 1921, it became a staple of Russian antisemitism, and made its way to Germany, where it became part of the Nazi literature of hate. In 1927, Henry Ford serialized it in his newspaper, the *Dearborn Independent*. He later recanted this as an error, but not before allowing it be additionally published in four volumes with running commentary.

In 1934, the Jewish community of Switzerland brought a legal action against the distributors of the *Protocols* in that country and were successful, as happened in South Africa a year earlier, and in 1993 in Russia as well. With the conclusion of the Second World War and the birth of the State of Israel, antisemites around the world supported its publication in many languages, and it remains even today among their "best sellers" not only in Arab countries opposed to Israel, but in Japan as well. With the rise of the "information explosion" on the Internet, copies are even more readily available for downloading free of charge in many of these same languages together with hideously antisemitic graphics either adapted directly from Nazi Julius Streicher's notorious newspaper *Der Sturmer* or created anew.

Thematic Lies of
the Protocols

―――――⧂⧂⧂――――――

Introduction: Thematic Lies of the Protocols

Appended to this chapter are two charts, the first entitled "Themes Addressed," and the second, "Central Ideas/Key Terms." Taken together, they constitute a veritable catalogue of the baseless charges against the Jewish people that have been the stock-in-trade of antisemites down through the centuries. Before addressing these charges, however, there are two questions which must be addressed here: (1) the necessity of such a document from the antisemite's perspective; and (2) the question of authorship, already addressed in Chapter One.

The "Necessity" of the Protocols

Although not all conspiracy theorists are antisemitic, contemporary and historical antisemites are linked by a common thread: the attribution to Jews of more political and economic power than is accurate, and of greater numbers than is true. Were this not enough, they are also joined together in their mistaken belief that, somehow, there exists a Jewish master plan for the subjugation and manipulation of the world's peoples, sight unseen until the appearance of the *Protocols*, a document that has almost mythic or sacred value for those who slavishly accept its supposed truths. Yet it was not until the nineteenth century, ironically, that such a document appeared, based on a French political satire rewritten to serve antisemitic ends. That it parallels the decline of the *ancien régime,* that is, the "old empire," is not surprising. For the nineteenth and twentieth centuries saw the nations of the Western world emerging into global competitive capitalism where it was personal and collective effort, rather than family ties or historic associations, that resulted in success, and, after 1789, the entrance of the Jews as near-equal players and partners to Christians in the economic enterprise. Couple this economic change with the political shift to various forms of participatory near-democracy in many places in Europe, and the world becomes a truly frightening place for the ordinary person. Add the economic and social dislocation, and the movement from rural agrarian and agricultural societies to city-centered industrial and production societies, and the world became ripe for such conspiracy theories, most especially when the collective ills of the new reality can be attributed to the one historical group already perceived as "different," "exotic," "strange," "outsiders," and worse (deicides, satanists): the Jews.

Thus, in an increasingly speeded-up world where communications and ever more sophisticated means of transmitting the written word becomes the norm, and where those frightened by the rapidity of change can draw upon a centuries-old tradition of antisemitic "us versus them" discourse ("them" = Jews), such a document would have had to be written! That its author, or authors, were able to uncover a nineteenth-century French political satire bearing no relationship whatsoever to either the Jewish people or the Jewish religious tradition and adapt it for avowedly anti-Jewish purposes is, in and of itself, bitterly and tragically ironic.

The Question of Authorship

To this day, no one knows for sure the nameless Russian individual or group of individuals who so perversely and successfully adapted Maurice Joly's 1864 satire *Dialogue aux Enfers entre Machiavel et Montesquieu, ou la politique aux xixe siècle* ("Conversation in Hell Between Machiavelli and Montesquieu, on the Politics of the Nineteenth Century"). It is assumed, however, that the French branch of the Okhrana, the Russian secret police and the forerunner of the notorious and equally antisemitic NKVD, was responsible for its adaptation and translation into Russian for transmittal back to the mother country, where it was presented to and rejected by Tsar Nicholas II, who was himself no friend of the Jews. Its public appearance as an appendix to the text of a book by Russian Orthodox priest Sergei Nilus, who died in disrepute, attracted little attention. It is only after the Russian Revolution of 1917, the flight of the White aristocracy to Germany, the connection with Nazi ideologue Alfred Rosenberg and with Adolf Hitler, that its dissemination and increasingly ill-gotten popularity begins in earnest—even though it was exposed as a forgery as early as 1921 and condemned in courts of law in 1933.

Thematic Lies

In the main, superior "street smarts" or native savvy, particularly in the area of economics, contempt for non-Jews who are to be used and abused as slaves, self-perceived status as chosen by God, elitism and superiority, Masonry and Freemasonry as Jewish front groups, and redefining the political institutions of the various European nation-states under the sovereignty of a "Jewish king/messiah" dominate the lies that form *The Protocols of the Learned Elders of Zion*. Although thoroughly refuted point for point in this document, these allegations remain, even today, sad to say, the bedrock of much of Western antisemitism. Why? Quite simply, because they readily lend themselves to the kind of anti-intellectual conspiratorial thinking, blaming of others for one's individual and group failures, and false perception of the world as "us versus them" that remain part of the baggage of an increasingly complex modernity. That which we have difficulty comprehending; that which is new, strange, or different from us; that which we simply do not like because it is not ours—all buy in to this mode of thinking, and, in the hands of masterful antisemitic manipulators, target both the Jews and the State of Israel in the aftermath of the Second World War as being beyond the pale of normal, decent society.

No one group in any society is in sole possession of the truth, and no minority group in any society deserves the enmity of the larger population because of its differences from the majority. The lies which are part-and-parcel of *The Protocols of the Learned Elders of Zion* could be all-too-easily adapted toward any relatively defenseless group that is disliked by political, religious, or economic leaders and which they see advantage in oppressing. From words of hate come deeds of hate; responsible societal involvement mandates rejecting such lies and calumnies, and, in the process, breaking the cycle of violence.

Themes Addressed

See original *Protocols* starting on page 143.

The Protocols of the Wise Men of Zion
CENTRAL IDEAS/KEY TERMS

Alcohol—1
Am Ha'aretz
Aristocracy—1, 3
Authority—1, 3, 5, 11, 15, 18,
    22
Chosen People—11, 14, 15
Churches—17
Clergy—17
Constitution—3, 10, 11
Credit—21
Debts—6, 21
Drunkenness—23
Education—3, 9, 10, 12, 16
Equality [Duty of]—1, 4, 9
Force—1, 3
Fraternity [Ideal of]—1, 9
Gentile Religion—14, 17
Gentiles—1, 3, 4, 5, 6, 7, 9, 10,
    11, 12, 13, 15, 16, 17, 18, 19,
    20, 21, 22
Gold—1, 15, 22
Government—1, 2, 3, 4, 5, 6, 7,
    8, 10, 11, 12, 13, 15, 16, 19, 20,
    21, 23, 24
Greed—1
House of King David—24
Industry—3, 4, 5, 6
Interest—21
Kahal—17
Law—1, 3, 5, 9, 11, 1, 15, 16, 17
Liberalism—1, 3, 5, 10, 15
Liberty [Light of]—1, 3, 4, 9, 12
Loans—20, 21
Masons; Masonry—11, 12, 15
Masses—1, 2, 3, 9, 10

Note to the Reader

Each of the following twenty-four (24) Protocols is arranged in the following manner: Both the "Outline" and the "Arguments" are taken directly from the actual texts themselves, using the translation by Victor Marsden, which is the most frequent English version of the Protocols. The "Refutations" are our specific responses to those false charges and lies as they present themselves in the Protocols, with sources and documentation supplied so that the reader can refer to them as desired. The authors believe that this thorough way of addressing the material makes this case for refutation beyond dispute and debate, finally laying to rest this too long-lived of antisemitic documents. The "Outlines" and "Arguments" are keyed to the original text of the Protocols as found in the "Appendix."

The titles "Protocols," "Protocols of the Elders of Zion," and "Protocols of the Learned Elders of Zion" are synonymous.

Protocol 1

The Basic Doctrine: "Right Lies in Might"

- Formulation of the system.
- Mankind essentially yields only to force.
- Political freedom is non-existent, and such an idea can only be used for political ends.
- A new authority succeeds a government weakened by liberal ideas.
- The power of gold has replaced faith.
- The masses are not guided by academic argument but by passions and sentiment.
- Politics and morals have nothing in common.
- Right lies in might.
- Do evil that good may come.
- Necessity overrules the moral.
- The masses are blind and led by upstarts who have no political sensibilities.
- Power and hypocrisy, violence and cunning, bribery and treason help to reach the goal and are therefore duties.
- Terrorism leads to blind submission.
- Prosperity and Gentile government.
- The abolition of privileges that were the last bulwark of the people.
- Greed and material desires stifle initiative.
- Any government may be changed like a pair of worn-out gloves.

Arguments

- Disregarding mere words and phrases, we will analyze the significance of every thought, and interpret events in the light of comparisons and deductions.
- It should be noted that people with evil instincts are more numerous than those with good ones; therefore, the best results in governing them are attained by intimidation and violence, and not by academic argument.
- What has controlled the wild animal called man?
- At the beginning of social organization, men submitted to

See original *Protocol* page 143.

brute force; later, they obeyed the law, which is the same force, only in a masked form.

- Political freedom is an idea, not a fact.
- In our times, the power of gold has become the substitute for the rulership of liberalism.
- Whether the government exhausts itself, or whether internal strife places it in the hands of external enemies, in either case it may be considered as irretrievably lost; it is in our power.
- I would ask the following question of him who, from a liberal heart, regards such arguments as unprincipled: if every government has two enemies and it is permissible to use all methods of warfare against the external enemy in ignorance of plans of attack and defense, in the use of night attack or attack by unequal forces, why should similar methods toward a worse foe, one who transgresses against social order and prosperity, be called unallowable or immoral?
- Can a sound and logical mind hope to govern successfully the masses by arguments and reasoning, when there is the possibility of counter-arguments, perhaps even stupid, but which nevertheless might present themselves as more agreeable to their superficial minds?
- Politics have nothing in common with morals.
- Our right lies in force.
- Where does it begin?
- In a government with poorly organized authority, in which the laws and the ruler are powerless amid the flood of rights ever multiplying out of liberalism, I find that there exists a new right: the right of the stronger to attack and destroy all existing regulations and statues, to take the law into his own hands, to change all institutions and become the ruler of those who give that right by yielding it voluntarily through their liberalism.
- With the present instability of all authority, our power will be more unassailable than any other, because it will be invisible until it has gained such strength that no cunning can undermine it.
- Out of the temporary evil to which we are now forced to resort will emerge the good of a permanent government, which will restore the orderly functioning of the mechanism of people's existence, now shaken by liberalism.

- In working out an expedient plan of action, it is necessary to take into consideration the meanness, the vacillation, the changeability of the crowd; its inability to appreciate and respect the conditions of individual life and well-being.
- Only the person educated from childhood for rulership can understand the words which are spelled with the letters of politics.
- The masses left to themselves, that is, to the direction of upstarts from among them, wreck themselves by party divisions created by the struggle for authority and honors, and the disorders arising therefrom.
- Only the plans of an autocrat can be laid out on a broad scale, clearly and in order, distributing everything properly in the mechanism of the government machinery.
- Look at these beasts, steeped in alcohol, stupefied by wine, the unlimited use of which is granted together with liberty.
- Our password is force and hypocrisy, for only force can conquer the realm of politics, especially if it is concealed in the talents essential to statesmen.
- Our government, following a line with peaceful conquest, has a right to substitute for the horrors of war less apparent and more effective executions of people, by which terrorism can be supported, thus bringing about blind submission.
- Already in ancient times, we were the first to shout the words "Liberty, Equality, Fraternity" among the people.
- Meanwhile, dynastic government has rested on this, the father passing on the knowledge of the course of political affairs to his son, so that nobody except the members of the dynasty understands, or could disclose such secrets to the people whom they ruled.
- From all ends of the world, the words "Liberty, Equality, Fraternity" brought whole legions into our ranks, through our blind agents carrying our flag with delight.
- On the ruins of the natural and hereditary aristocracy of the Gentiles we have set up the aristocracy of our educated classes and over all the aristocracy of money.
- Our triumph has also been made easier because, in our relations with the people necessary to us, we have always played

upon the most sensitive strings of the human mind—on calculation, greed, and the insatiable material desires of men.

• The abstract conception of liberty made it possible for us to convince the crowd that government is only the management for the owner of the country, the people, and that the steward can be changed like a pair of worn-out gloves.

Refuting Protocol 1

The false premise of the first protocol, that "Right lies in Might," is predicated upon the following erroneous assumptions: (1) That both freedom and liberty are myths; that these myths were created by the Jews, who use them to dupe the unsuspecting and easily deceivable masses; (2) that the authority and power of government are self-serving, designed to promote the interests of those already in power; and (3) that gold (money) is the primary tool used to subvert the will of these largely ignorant and easily led masses.

While such a contemptuous and contemptible view of the ordinary citizen has a long and dishonorable history in Western civilization, an examination of the texts of the Jewish religious tradition, primarily the Torah, Midrash, and Talmud, leads one to the very opposite conclusions, namely: (1) that freedom and liberty are the very foundations of any healthy society and are rooted in Judaism (traced back to the historical experience of the Israelites during the Egyptian enslavement); (2) that government exists to serve the needs of the people, and that those in positions of power and authority have a responsibility not only to their constituencies but to God as well; and (3) that gold (or money) is, indeed, a tool, valued not only for its aesthetic value, but especially for the good it can do for humanity.

Turning first to the text of the Holy Scriptures, called Torah in the Jewish religious tradition, and second to that encyclopedic resource of historical Jewish knowledge, the Babylonian Talmud, and finally, where appropriate, to the various biblical commentaries, we find that that there is no verse more significant than Leviticus 25:10, "Proclaim liberty throughout the land unto all the inhabitants" (all biblical citations, unless otherwise noted, are from the Jewish Publication Society's English translation). Originating in the context of the celebration of the Jubilee Year, these words have inspired freedom-loving people throughout the ages. Significantly, it was this verse that was chosen by the United States in the celebration of its Bicentennial (1976) and appears on the Liberty Bell in Philadelphia.

Second, much of the evolution of the Jewish religious tradition bases its religious and moral-ethical values on the enslavement in Egypt, and the subsequent liberation and entry into the Promised Land of Israel. This affects how Jews act both in their own community and with those outside it. Exodus 10:3 dramatically addresses the importance of the desire for freedom and liberty in God's demand to Egypt's Pharaoh through Moses and his brother Aaron: "Let My people go that they may worship Me." This command is the basis of the Passover holiday, observed by Jews throughout the centuries and all over the world, where the words "In every generation one is obligated to see oneself as one who personally went out from Egypt" (*Family Participation Haggadah*, p. 114) are repeated every year. It is this understanding, too, that governed Isaiah's sense of prophetic mission:

> The spirit of the Lord God is upon me;
> Because the Lord has anointed me
> He has sent me as a herald of joy to the humble
> To bind up the wounded of heart
> To proclaim release (liberty) to the captives,
> Liberty to the imprisoned.

> (Isaiah 61:1)

Another example of the importance of liberty and freedom from the Scriptures is Jeremiah's report regarding Zedekiah, king of Judah in Jerusalem: "The word which came to Jeremiah from the Lord, after the king Zedekiah had made a covenant with all the people in Jerusalem, to proclaim liberty among them; that everyone should set free his Hebrew slaves, both male and female, and that no one should keep his fellow Judean enslaved" (Jeremiah 34:8–9). Then, too, the author(s) of the Book of Proverbs declared that "when the righteous are in authority, the people rejoice; but when the wicked rule, the people groan" (29:2).

Respect for law and the legal system have long been hallmarks of Jewish life. Governmental officials, particularly judges, are seen as God's representatives, and carry the weighty responsibility to act justly. The Torah commands the Israelites to "appoint magistrates and officials for your tribes, in all the settlements the Lord your God is giving you, and they shall govern the people with due justice. You shall not judge unfairly; you shall show no partiality; you shall not take bribes, for bribes blind the eyes of the discerning and upset the pleas of the just. Justice, justice shall you pursue"(Deuteronomy 16:18–20). The law is a divine gift and commitment to justice a divine imperative. No one, not even a king of Israel, is above the law of ancient Israel (witness the prophet Nathan's rebuke to King David about his questionable relationship with Bathsheba and his arranging of her husband Uriah's death, II Samuel 12:1–15). The ancient rabbis illustrated this commitment to law by having God say, "Would that they had forsaken Me but kept My law" (Proem to Lamentations Rabbah, ed. Soncino, p. 2).

A well-known talmudic statement emphasizes the respect for legal authority by declaring, "The law of the government is law" (BT Gittin 10a). The rabbis also interpreted the following quotation from Scripture as indicating that the Jewish tradition regards the rule of law and respect for the government as the dividing line between civilization and chaos: Habakkuk 1:14 states: "You have made mankind like the fish of the sea, Like creeping things that have no ruler." The Talmud's explanation is: "Just as among fish of the sea, the greater swallow up the smaller ones, so with men, were it not for the fear of the government, men would swallow each other alive. This is just what we learned: Rabbi Hanina, the deputy high priest, said, "Pray for the welfare of the government, for were it not for the fear thereof, men would swallow each other alive" (BT Avodah Zarah 4a, ed. Soncino, p. 12).

The Mishnah (Avot 3:2), commenting on Jeremiah 29:7 ("And seek the welfare of the city to which I have exiled you and pray to the Lord in its behalf; for in its prosperity you shall prosper") teaches that Jews should pray for the welfare of the government wherever they live. The medieval French authority Rabbi Menahem Meiri stressed that "this is intended not merely in behalf of a Jewish government, but on behalf of Gentile ones too" (cited in Judah Goldin, *The Living Talmud: The Wisdom of the Fathers*, p. 120). This is the source for the prayer for the welfare of the local government, a prayer that Jews said even in the early days of Nazi Germany and in present-day Iran where they also face persecution.

Gentiles who lived among the ancient Israelites were subject to the same moral-ethical commandments required of every Israelite. According to the great twelfth-century authority Maimonides, "A heathen who accepts the seven commandments and observes them scrupulously is a righteous heathen and will have a portion in the world to come" (*Mishneh Torah*, Melakim 8:11, cited in I. Twersky, *Introduction to the Code of Maimonides*, p. 455). Later, the so-called seven Noahide laws—the prohibitions of idolatry, blasphemy, bloodshed, sexual sins, theft, eating from a living animal, and establishing a legal system (Genesis Rabbah, Noah 34:8, on Genesis 9:7, ed. Soncino, p. 272)—were understood to be the basic obligatory statutes which must undergird any civil society. Only Gentiles who rejected this basic social contract were considered outlaws.

Lastly, already in the Book of Proverbs, gold (money) is understood to be a desirable and usable commodity, but not one that should dominate and control the individual. "How much better to acquire wisdom than gold/To acquire understanding is preferable to silver" (16:16); "Gold is plentiful, jewels abundant/But wise speech is a precious object" (20:15); "Repute is preferable to great wealth/Grace is better than silver and gold" (22:1).

Historically, the liberated Israelites brought their precious metals under the direction of the artist Bezalel to beautify the House of God, but never perceived such wealth as an end in itself (Exodus 31 ff.). Rabbinic literature stressed this theme: "Gold and silver take a man out of this world and the world to come, but the Torah brings a man to the life of the world to come" (Sifre Num., ed. Horovitz, Korah 119 f., 39b, p. 144). In the medieval period, Rabbi Judah the Pious wrote, "If a man should ask: 'Behold, I have money; shall I buy a scroll of the Torah for it, or shall I distribute it to the destitute poor?' Answer him with the words of Isaiah, 'When you see the naked, clothe him'" (Isaiah 58:7). Thus, generations of Jews were taught that money has to be used for the betterment of people, and not for selfish or egotistical purposes. To the rabbis, wealthy people are judged on how well they use their wealth to help others. Witness the three wealthy families of Jerusalem that were remembered for supplying the entire city with its needs while it was under siege by the Romans (BT Gittin 56a, ed. Soncino, p. 256).

Summary

The fictions of Protocol 1 are easily refuted by reference to biblical texts and to postbiblical Jewish literature. Historically, freedom and liberty were and remain Jewish ideals, not only for Jews, but for all of humanity. Those charged with the authority and power of government bear the moral-ethical and Divinely commanded responsibility to govern wisely and well with the support of the governed.

Gentiles were expected to live up to the same ethical norms as the Israelites. These ethical norms were summarized in the seven Noahide laws. Only people who rejected the basic social norms were considered outlaws. Lastly, gold (money) is to be used in the service of humanity and never to be accumulated as a goal in itself.

Protocol 2

Economic War and Disorganization
Lead to International Government

Outline

- War, shifted from a territorial to an economic basis, thus eliminating frontiers, will finally result in the establishment of an international government.
- The use of untrained and servile administrators as camouflage for trained specialists and talented advisers.
- Gentiles are uncritical and guided by routine: "Let them live to amuse themselves or in the past!"
- Disorganizing effects of Darwinism, Marxism, and Nietzscheism.
- Political action, to be successful, must suit the temperament of the people.
- The press is a great modern force in which free speech is triumphant, but it has fallen into our hands.
- "It has gathered for us influence and gold while we remain in the shadow."

Arguments

- It is indispensable for our purposes that, as far as possible, wars should bring no territorial advantage.
- The administrators chosen by us from the masses for their servility will not be persons trained for government, and consequently they will easily become pawns in our game, played by our learned and talented councillors, specialists educated from early childhood to administer world affairs.
- Do not think that these statements are empty words.
- It is essential that we take into consideration contemporary ideas and the character of peoples, in order to avoid mistakes in policy and in guiding administrative affairs.
- There is one great force in the hands of modern governments, which creates thought movements among the people; that is, the press.

See original *Protocol* page 151.

• The return has been worth the price, though we have sacrificed many of our own people.

Refuting Protocol 2

In addition to the supposed contempt for Gentiles refuted in the response to the first protocol, and the false allegation of gold or money as the primary means of motivating the masses (also refuted above), the second protocol adds two additional lies to the book's spurious arsenal: (1) that a so-called master plan exists that involves an international economic and political conspiracy on the part of the Jewish people, especially its leaders, to subjugate the peoples of the world, especially the Western world, and (2) that the press (and by extension all other media) is a tool in the hands of these conspirators. Again, both biblical tradition and Jewish history refute these charges.

What lies behind the first allegation is a pessimistic view of humanity that arose in the nineteenth century. This view transferred Charles Darwin's theory of the evolution of species onto the plane of human history. Known as Social Darwinism, it saw conflict between nation-states and peoples paralleling that of the animal kingdom, whereby stronger communities would best weaker ones, and only the fittest among the continuously evolving human societies would survive. Indeed, Adolf Hitler advocated this position only too well in urging his fantasy "superior Germanic nation" forward to conquer the world and destroy its main enemy, the Jews (along with their other victims in their murderous quest). The horrors of World War II and the genocidal events of the Nazi Holocaust are well known and need not be recited here. Suffice it to say that this worldview flies in the face of a true biblical understanding of what human beings are and can become.

Creation, as it is presented to us in the early chapters of the first book of the biblical text, Genesis, affirms that humanity is the very apex of God's creative endeavors. Thus, in the first recording of the creation, after having created evening and morning; firmament and dry land; grass, herbs, and trees; sun and moon; and sea and land creatures, on the sixth day humanity is created as the very climax of the entire process, and God, in a "reflective" moment, surveys the Divine handiwork and perceives it as "very good." The Rabbis used this text to teach of the value of each individual human being. "Therefore," they said, "but a single man was created in the world, to teach that if any man has caused a single soul to perish, Scripture imputes it to him as if he had caused a whole world to perish . . . and if any man alive saves a single soul, [it is] as though he has saved alive a whole world" (Genesis 1:26–31; M. Sanhedrin 4:5, ed. Danby, p. 388). Humanity, created in God's Divine image, is presented as the pinnacle of the creative process. The enduring power of this teaching can be seen in the words of Rabbi Abraham Joshua Heschel, first published in 1963. Heschel wrote: "The Bible does not say, God created the plant or the animal; it says, God created different kinds of plants, different kinds of animals (Gen, 1:11–12, 21–25). In striking contrast, it does not say, God created different kinds of man, men of different colors and races, it proclaims God created one single man. From one single man all men are descended. To think of man in terms of white, black or yellow is more than an error. It is an eye disease, a cancer of the soul" (Heschel, "Religion and Race," in *The Insecurity of Freedom*, pp. 86–87). Heschel summed up: "Racial or religious bigotry must be recognized for what it is: satanism, blasphemy" (ibid., p. 86). Teachings about the equality and individuality of all people can also be found all throughout Rabbinic literature.

Jewish tradition has consistently regarded the human being in the most positive of lights. Possessing a dual nature, consisting of a good inclination and a bad inclination, created in "the image of God," but a creature made out of dust and ashes, humanity remains, at the very same time, "little less than the angels." Thus, from the Jewish perspective the human being, despite its flaws and imperfections, is seen positively, filled with potential to be God's partner. And when people act righteously, they come close to fulfilling this potential. According to the rabbinic description. "Every judge who judges with complete fairness . . . [it is] as though he has become a partner to the Holy One, blessed be He, in the creation" (BT, Shabbat 10a, ed. Soncino, p. 35).

Every human is endowed with the ability to make the right choice when confronted with the conflicts and ambiguities of any age, as poignantly expressed in Deuteronomy 30:19–20:

> I call heaven and earth to witness against you this day: I have put before you life and death, blessing and curse; Choose life, if you and your offspring would live; by loving the Lord your God, heeding His commandments, and holding fast to Him; For thereby you shall have life.

We turn to the second wrong assumption of the second protocol, the manipulative use of the press (and other media). Such a contemptuous view of journalism flies in the face of Jewish history and the values reflected in the history of modern Jewish journalism, from the first Jewish newspaper published in Amsterdam, Holland, in 1675 to the more than 300-year history of Jewish involvement and integrity in newspaper publishing throughout the world.

In addition, one finds no support whatsoever in Jewish sources, history, or experience for the use of the press as a tool of the politically or economically powerful over the weaker, either within or outside the Jewish community. The biblical command to "Keep far from a false charge; do not bring death on the innocent and righteous, for I will not acquit the wrongdoer" (Exodus 23:7) set the tone for the Jewish perspective.

Historically, it should also be noted that the organized Jewish communities rarely practiced censorship of the written word. When they did, it was usually where the material was of a morally questionable nature or understood to represent an attack upon the Jewish people or Jewish religious tradition. These actions, imposed only on members of the community, were taken in defense of a community that lived in a minority and constantly threatened status.

The above points must also be applied to issues of freedom of speech and the relatively open position of Jewish religious tradition except where the intent is slander or defamation. Contrary positions and points of view are found throughout Jewish literature, and most especially in the encyclopedic Talmuds of Judaism (both the Babylonian and the Palestinian) as well as throughout the vast biblical commentary literature. Just how highly the rabbis of the Talmud expressed their respect for the concept of open debate and exchange of differing views is found in the description of how the school of Shammai and the school of Hillel disputed each other, both declaring "the law is like us." Finally, a voice was heard from Heaven: "Both are the words of the living God, but the law is in agreement with the rulings of the school of Hillel" (BT Eruvin 13b, ed. Soncino, pp. 85–86). A modern theologian, Eliezer Berkovits, described how this process works: "the various interpretations and . . . decisions were left to the teachers of each generation" (Berkovits, *Not in Heaven*, pp. 52–53). Thus, opposing positions could be aired, but ultimately a practical decision was reached so that the people would know how to translate the discussion from theory to practice.

Protocol 3

Methods of Conquest

Outline

- "Things Near at Hand," the goal.
- Authority built on terrorism.
- Rulers and masses cannot combine.
- Authorities taught to abuse their power.
- Unlimited oratory.
- Attacks on administrative personnel.
- Constitutions now include fictitious and not actual rights.
- The proletarian is a slave either to his economic master or his comrades.
- Aristocracy, the natural protector of the people, now destroyed.
- Extending pretended help under the guise of socialism, anarchy, and communism.
- Famine and malnutrition give capital the power over the worker, and therein lies Jewish power.
- Teaching the science of the construction of human society.
- Equality cannot exist.
- Suffering to be abolished by diminishing the discrepancy between education and work.
- Hatred toward superior classes.
- "The One Big Strike."
- The French Revolution.
- Repeated disappointment of the masses.
- An unconquerable international force.
- The word "Liberty" pushes society into a struggle against all authority.

Arguments

- I can tell you today that our goal is close at hand.
- Contemporary constitutional balances will soon break down, for we have set them unevenly in order that they may not cease to fluctuate and wear out their supports.

See original *Protocol* page 153.

- To induce ambitious persons to abuse their power, we have set all forces in opposition, one against another, after developing their liberal tendencies toward independence.
- Irrepressible speech-makers have changed parliamentary sessions and administrative meetings into oratorical controversies.
- The masses are condemned more surely to heavy labor by poverty than they were by slavery and serfdom.
- Under our guidance, the masses have destroyed the aristocracy that was their natural protector and nurse, and whose interests were indissolubly bound up with the well-being of the people.
- We will represent ourselves as the saviors of the laboring classes who have come to liberate them from this oppression by suggesting that they join our army of socialists, anarchists, communists, to whom we always extend our help, under the guise of fraternal principles of the universal human solidarity of our social masonry.
- Hunger gives the power to capital over the worker more truly than did royal authority by law give it to the aristocracy.
- Throughout want and the jealous hatreds engendered by it, we manipulate the masses and eliminate those who stand in our way.
- When the time comes for our universal ruler to be crowned, the same hands will sweep away all that may oppose him.
- The Gentiles have lost the power of thinking without our scientific counsel.
- The true science of social structure, the secret of which we conceal from the Gentiles, would demonstrate to all that position and labor must be kept in their separate spheres so as not to cause human suffering through lack of coordination between education and manual work.
- This hostility will be still more accentuated as the result of crises that will close stock exchange operations and stop the wheels of industry.
- They will not touch our people, because we shall know beforehand the moment of attack and will take measures to protect our own.

- We have convinced the Gentiles that "progress" is leading all to a reign of reason.
- When the people realize that all kinds of concessions and lenience are made to them in the name of liberty, they imagine that they are the masters, and endeavor to grasp power.
- Since then, we have led the people from one disappointment to another in order to make them renounce even us in favor of that ruler of Zionist blood whom we are preparing for the world.
- Being an international force, we are at present invulnerable, because if we are attacked by one government, other governments will uphold us.
- How to explain such a phenomenon, such an illogical attitude on the part of the masses toward events that seem to be of the same order?
- The word "Liberty" goads human society into a struggle against all authority, even that of God or of Nature.

Refuting Protocol 3

The most antisemitic of the three protocols encountered thus far, the third presents to the unsuspecting reader a view of the Jewish people as arrogant and corrupt, a view totally at variance with the realities of Jewish history and the teachings of the Jewish religious tradition. What lies behind this false assumption is the long-standing misreading of the biblical traditions of chosenness and election. It also ignores the long-standing Jewish tradition of public service to the larger community and the equally significant responsibility of rabbinic authority within the Jewish community.

First, let us consider the alleged arrogance of the Jewish people. Arrogance is the very opposite of humility, and it is humility which characterizes the greatest Jewish role model and the most revered figure of the Jewish Scriptures, Moses. It was Moses, according to Jewish tradition, who attained the highest degree of prophecy and experienced the closest relationship to the Divine, and yet saw himself as unworthy and flawed. Indeed, his acknowledgment of his supposed speech defect caused him to implore God to accept his older brother Aaron as the spokesper-son for Israel, as well as for God, in their series of confrontations with the Pharaoh of Egypt. So self-effacing was Moses that the Bible characterized him thus: "Now Moses was a very humble man, more so than any other man on earth" (Numbers 12:3).

The prophets of ancient Israel, especially Isaiah, Jeremiah, and Ezekiel, consistently condemned arrogance and championed the value of humility. But it is the prophet Micah who captures the essence of Jewish humility when he presents it as one of the fundamental principles of the Jewish religious tradition: "He has told you, O man, what is good, and what the Lord requires of you: Only to do justice, and to love goodness, and to walk modestly with your God" (Micah 6:8). Together with the psalm-ist's words in Psalm 51:17, "True sacrifice to God is a contrite spirit; God, you will not despise a contrite and crushed heart," we see here the core ideal of how Jews are to behave modestly in their dealings with all their fellow human beings.

Running throughout the Holy Scriptures is the Jewish peo-ple's self-understanding that it has been chosen by God as a special act of love, and not through any special merit of its own. Along with this selection comes a special responsibility to serve as God's collective witness to the reality of the Divine Presence in the world. Joshua, Moses' successor, is very specific about this: "You are witnesses against yourselves that you have . . . chosen to serve the Lord" (Joshua 24:22). By "serve" is meant to scrupu-lously perform the ethical-moral and ritual-ceremonial acts that are the essence of true Jewish religious duty. Indeed, not by vir-tue of economic strength, military prowess, political astuteness, or size of population was the Jewish people chosen to enter into a covenant with God, as is verified in Deuteronomy 7:7–8: "It is not because you are the most numerous of peoples that the Lord set His heart on you and chose you—indeed, you are the small-est of peoples; but it was because the Lord loved you and kept the oath He made to your fathers."

It is much more accurate, therefore, to describe the unique relationship between the Jewish people and God by saying that just as God chose the Jewish people to enter into the covenantal relationship, so, too, did the Jewish people choose to affirm both God and its selection and to act responsibly by its observance of the commandments and commitments spelled out in great detail and depth throughout the Scriptures. Thus, for Jews, the concept of chosenness leads to responsibilities before privilege, as seen in God's words to Israel through the prophet Amos: "You alone have I singled out of all the families of the earth—That is why I will call you to account for all your iniquities" (Amos 3:2).

By extension, therefore, those who find themselves in positions of communal responsibility carry additional measures of trust. Based upon the Bible's insights, they are viewed as if they were judges, who, along with parents, are God's special representatives and must, therefore, accept an even more stringent code of behavior.

Deuteronomy 1:16–17 states this most clearly:

Hear out your fellow men, and decide justly between any man and a fellow Israelite or a stranger. You shall not respect persons in judgment; you shall hear the small and the great alike; you shall not be partial in judgment, hear out low and high alike. Fear no man, for judgment is God's.

Maimonides, in his great code, the *Mishneh Torah*, elaborated this theme, listing the attributes required of judges, including being "strong in the performance of the commandments and strict with themselves, [in] control of their passions, [with a] character above reproach. . . . And, just as Moses our teacher was humble, so every judge should be humble" (cited in Twersky, *Introduction to the Code of Maimonides*, p. 147).

The same is applicable not only for those in political office in the larger society, but for rabbinical leaders within the Jewish community. What is paramount in all such discussions in both biblical and postbiblical literature is the genuine and evident respect demanded of those who come into contact with those holding office, whether Jewish or non-Jewish. Anything less, says Jewish tradition, is an abdication of moral and ethical responsibility on the part of Jews individually and the Jewish people collectively. This view, long a part of Jewish identity and self-definition, stands in clear and direct contradiction to the third protocol.

Protocol 4

The Destruction of Religion by Materialism

Outline

- All republics pass through several phases: the first is that of "senseless ravings"; then appears that of "demagogy which breeds anarchy," and this finally becomes a despotism which through its secret character remains unknown to the people.
- The laws of existence establish servitude, and therefore they are contradictory to liberty, free from belief in God or the brotherhood of man, and exclude the thought of equality.
- Religion must therefore be undermined to be replaced by materialism.
- The enemy common to all will be forgotten by directing the attention of the Gentiles to trade and industry, which eventually, to be disorganized, must be put on a speculative basis.
- Highly developed industrial life has evolved a cold and heartless society, which has a true cult for gold and material pleasures.
- The lower classes of the Gentiles will join us against the intellectual Gentiles.

Arguments

- Every republic passes through several stages.
- Who and what can overthrow this invisible power?
- Liberty, even, would be harmless and coexist with a governmental program without injury to the welfare of the people if it were based on the principle of belief in God and on the brotherhood of man, but excluded the idea of equality, which is contradicted by the very laws of existence that establish submission to authority.
- To divert Gentile thought and observation, interest must be deflected to industry and commerce.
- The intense struggle for supremacy and the hard knocks of economic life have already created, and will continue to create, a society which is disillusioned, cold, and heartless.

See original *Protocol* page 159.

Refuting Protocol 4

The fourth protocol pictures industrialization, commerce, and business as "cold and heartless," and the Gentiles employed by Jews as little more than slaves. Highly technological and industrialized modern societies, collectively ruled by the supposed Jewish international network, are the antithesis of freedom, equality, and brotherhood.

Nothing could be further from a true Jewish understanding than the lies perpetrated in the fourth protocol.

First, let us trace the history and mores of Jewish attitudes toward business and commerce. Jewish involvement in business, commerce, and the like has a long and honorable history, beginning with ancient Israel's having served as a commercial highway between Egypt on the south, the Arabian Peninsula to the east, and Phoenicia, Syria, and Mesopotamia to the north. Early biblical and rabbinic law reflects the fact that Jews originally lived in an agrarian society. After the Roman destruction of the Second Temple in the year 70, and the spread of Jews throughout the Diaspora, in the West commercial ventures rather than agriculture became the primary mode of economic sustenance for Jewish communities. Often this was the result of secular and ecclesiastical laws that forbade Jewish ownership of land. As a result they were forced to rely upon sources of income and trade that provided easy access to liquid capital. For reasons of safety and security, Jews gravitated to such commercial enterprises as the spice trade, jewelry, gold, silver, and precious stones, clothing and textiles, the fur trade, brokering, and banking. Inevitably, some of these activities led to stresses and strains in relationships between Jews and non-Jews. It was only with the significant lessening of antisemitism in the West, especially in the United States, that Jews were able to expand beyond their portable commercial ventures into settled establishments, businesses, and property.

Wherever Jews have found themselves throughout history, their economic activity was based on a strong religious understanding about the ethics of the pursuit of economic goals. Such pursuits are valid and legitimate in God's world. An entire chapter of the Pentateuch (Leviticus 25) is devoted to business law and ethics, and other laws are interspersed throughout the Torah (Exodus 21–23, Leviticus 19, Deuteronomy 22–25).

According to the Bible, Jewish business activities must be governed by a sense of moral and ethical obligation, individual and corporate, to both the individual employee and the greater society. Violations of trust in business dealings are understood to be transgressions against God, and deceitful business practices undermine the moral order of things. The rabbis of the Talmud considered that robbery was so great a crime that it had precipitated the Flood in Noah's time. "R. Johanan said: Come and see how great is the power of robbery, for lo, though the generation of the flood transgressed all laws, their decree of punishment was sealed only because they stretched out their hands to rob" (BT Sanhedrin 108a, ed. Soncino, p. 740). Mismanagement of economic resources in business, the exploitation of workers, and ecological abuse of the physical environment are all understood to be breaches of trust between humanity and God. (An excellent summary of Jewish business ethics is provided by the *Encyclopaedia Judaica*.)

There is a distinctive Jewish ethical framework for the conduct of business within which Jews have always operated. This framework regards wealth as a gift from God, legitimate and useful, but operative within the parameters laid down by Jewish law, morality, and custom. These parameters forbid the earning of wealth through dishonest means, which include not only theft, but coercion, misrepresentation, unrevealed conflict of interest, and defective merchandise. These ethics reject the concept of "let the buyer beware," and place the onus for full disclosure on the seller. Corporations have the same moral obligations as shareholders, and therefore what is not permissible for the individual is also forbidden to the corporation.

As a result of the national orientation of Judaism, the group and society have, as it were, a share in the wealth of the individual. Private property rights are recognized and protected but are never absolute. This means that possessors of wealth, corporate or otherwise, can be taxed to meet the social needs of the community, whether these include charity for poor and inefficient citizens or the unemployed, or the provision of public services.

Furthermore, business may not be conducted in such a way as

will damage another's property or health, or, for that matter, the ecological quality of life of other individuals or of society.

It is worthwhile to examine the evolution of Jewish attitudes toward slavery. To be sure, the Hebrew Bible reflects Israelite ownership of both Hebrew and non-Hebrew slaves, though both Exodus 21:2 and Deuteronomy 15:12 make strikingly clear that the former are to remain in servitude for only six years and be released during the seventh, the Jubilee. Additionally, Hebrew slaves may only become so by order of the court as punishment for thievery (Exodus 22:2) or voluntarily because of a failure to repay debts (Leviticus 25:39, Proverbs 22:7, II Kings 4:1, Isaiah 50:1, Amos 2:6, 8:6, Nehemiah 5:5).

Non-Israelite slaves may be purchased outright (Leviticus 25:44–45) or captured in war (Numbers 31:26–27, Deuteronomy 20:10–11), and remain so in perpetuity or when released at the discretion of their owners.

In both cases, the master has the obligation to treat such individuals properly and with respect, as they are considered members of his extended household according to both Leviticus 25 and Deuteronomy 23 and dramatically in Jeremiah 34.

In the postbiblical or talmudic period, many of the discussions regarding Hebrew and non-Hebrew slaves reflect the orientations already expressed in the Scriptures. The treatment of slaves was so strictly regulated that the Talmud declared: "Whoever buys a Hebrew slave is like buying a master for himself" (BT Kiddushin 20a, ed. Soncino, p. 91). However, because of historical conditions, particularly in Western society, Jewish ownership of slaves ceased early on. Thus the discussions are essentially theoretical or based on earlier circumstances.

What is more important and reflects both the biblical and post-biblical attitudes is the concept of compassion for all humanity. It was God's compassionate love that enabled him to enter into the original covenant at Mount Sinai with the Children of Israel (see, for example, Psalm 78:38, Exodus 33:19, Deuteronomy 8:18, Isaiah 9:16). The prophets are concerned with the plight of the widow, the fatherless, the poor, and the orphan, and the responsibility of the House of Israel to address these moral-ethical inequalities and provide welfare relief for those who so desperately needed it. By extension, what was and is applicable for the smaller, self-contained society of Jews is understood to be applicable to the larger non-Jewish society. As the talmudic rabbis put it, for "the sake of peace" Jews who live in a mixed society should help take care of the Gentile poor, bury their dead, and comfort their mourners (Tosefta Gittin, ed. S. Lieberman, 3:13, p. 259, author's translation).

Thus, the contempt for both Gentiles and workers expressed in the fourth protocol is very much at variance with Jewish thinking, religious tradition, and historical experience. In addition, there continues to be a strong ethical thrust in Judaism regarding all business relationships, together with a view of commerce and industrialization as among the benefits of a world created by God and given to humanity to partner in its ongoing development.

Protocol 5

Despotism and Modern Progress

Outline

- Planning a strong central government for countries in which "morality is now sustained by police measures."
- Mechanical regulation of all forms of government function and social life.
- Despotism and modern progress are not incompatible.
- Idea of "personal rights" inspired among the people, disintegrating social discipline, and then authority becomes public property.
- Government of the masses by "cunningly constructed theories and phrases" devised by "our administrative specialists."
- The Jesuits and Catholics.
- A "coalition of Gentiles against us" is not possible owing to dissensions among them as personal and national interests have been brought into conflict by stirring up religious and racial hatreds.
- Omnipotence of this secret power.

Arguments

- What form of administration can be given to a society in which corruption has permeated everywhere, where riches are obtained only by sharp practice and fraudulent methods, where dissoluteness reigns, where morality is maintained by police measures and severe laws, not by voluntary acceptance of principle, and where the spirit of internationalism has eliminated devotion to country and religion?
- When people regarded rulers as manifestations of God's will, they subjected themselves to the autocracy of monarchs without a murmur, but as soon as we inspired in them the idea of their personal rights, they began to regard rulers simply as mortals.
- A world coalition of the Gentiles could cope with us temporarily, but we are ensured against this by roots of dissension amongst them so deep that they cannot be torn out.

See original *Protocol* page 161.

- *Per ME reges regunt*—"through Me shall kings reign."
- All the wheels of the government mechanism are driven by the motor which is in our hands, and that motor is—gold.
- Capital, in order that it may operate without interference, must secure freedom to monopolize industry and trade.
- The most important problem of our government is to weaken the mind of society by criticism, to dissociate this mind from thought which creates opposition, to deflect mental effort into mere empty eloquence.
- We will adopt for ourselves the liberal side of all parties and all movements, and provide orators who will talk so much that they will tire the people by their speeches until they turn from orators in disgust.
- To obtain control over public opinion, it is first necessary to confuse it by the expression from various sides of so many conflicting opinions that the Gentiles will lose themselves in the labyrinth and come to understand that it is best to have no opinion on political questions, which it is not given to society at large to understand, but only to the ruler who directs society.
- There is nothing more dangerous than private initiative if it has a touch of genius, for it can accomplish more than millions of people among whom we have sown dissension.
- We will wear out and exhaust the Gentiles by all this so that they will be compelled to offer us an international authority, which by its position will enable us to absorb without disturbance all the governmental forces of the world and thus form a super-government.

Refuting Protocol 5

We have already addressed a number of the themes that appear in this chapter (Jewish views of government, gold [or money], and Gentiles). Therefore, let us turn instead to the two issues that undergird this and all of the previous protocols: (1) Jewish ethics, and (2) the Jewish relationship to the larger society.

A proper Jewish understanding of humanity's ethical foundation directly relates to God and the divine expectation of how relationships between people must be conducted. The Mishnah teaches: "For transgressions that are between man and God, the Day of Atonement effects atonement; but for transgressions that are between man and his fellow, the Day of Atonement effects atonement only if he has appeased his fellow" (Mishnah Yoma 8:9, ed. Danby, p. 172). For Jews, ethical behavior is inextricably bound up with religious ritual and ceremonial behavior, each containing within itself the seeds of the other. Yet it is the ethical which mandates the Bible's concerns with human behavior: The prophet Micah (6:8) reminds Israel that "He has told you, O man, what is good, And what the Lord requires of you: Only to do justice, And to love goodness, And to walk modestly with your God," while Deuteronomy 16:20 demands: "Justice, justice shall you pursue, that you may thrive and occupy the land that the Lord your God is giving you." The prophet Amos (5:15) cries out: "Hate evil and love good and establish justice in the gate." In Genesis 18:19, Abraham is told, "to instruct his children and posterity to keep the way of the Lord by doing what is just and right." These are but a few of the many examples which resound through the Bible.

The belief in the ability of every person to constantly improve his or her moral station, along with the tacit divine command that each person try to do so, has been a mainstay of Judaism from biblical days to contemporary times. Much of Jewish religious literature is concerned with enumerating specific ethical responsibilities toward the less fortunate, such as the widow, the orphan, the fatherless, and the poor (e.g., Deuteronomy 15:7–11). Even celebrations had to include the disenfranchised and downtrodden, as was commanded in the Book of Esther (9:22): "They were to observe them as days of feasting and merrymaking, and as an occasion of sending gifts to one another and presents to the poor." Isaiah (58:3) summed up this sense of responsibility: "It is to share your bread with the hungry, and to take the wretched poor into your home; When you see the naked, to clothe him." The famous rabbinic exemplar Hillel (1st cent. B.C.E.) is quoted as saying, "What is hateful to you, do not do to your neighbor; that is the whole Torah, while the rest is commentary thereof; go and learn it" (BT Shabbat 31a, ed. Soncino p. 140).

What is additionally significant to ancient Israel's conception of ethics and morality was its realization that both the individual and society stand the best chance for success if the behaviors embodied in the laws that they enacted were recognized as based on divine intent. Today, most Jews still believe that individual and society both function best as they embody their most cherished ethical and moral ideals in legal statutes and ordinances. The legal material found in the encyclopedic Talmuds of Palestine and Babylonia maintains a constant focus on the specific, the "do's" and "do not's" of particular societal situations and their legal resolution even in the midst of the most theoretical discussions.

Throughout the entire span of Jewish history, "righteousness" has been the term which best epitomizes the highest ethical values and behaviors. The just individual is the righteous individual, and a just society is a righteous society. This view is not confined to the Jewish realm: In an important commentary to one of the sections of the Babylonian Talmud, we find the following statement: "The righteous among the gentiles have a share in the world to come" (Tosefta Sanhedrin 13:3, author's translation). Thus, for Judaism, ethics and morality are not believed to be the sole possession of either ancient or contemporary Israel; proper behavior toward one's fellow human beings is the responsibility of all humanity, and all who pursue the ethical can share in the eternal reward.

Not only citizens were included in this mandate of responsibility, but leaders as well. For example, in ancient Israel the king was understood to be under a divine mandate of ethical and moral responsibility (Deuteronomy 14:20). Like others charged with administrative and judicial obligations, the kings of ancient Israel were to lead their people justly, that is, righteously (I Samuel 12:14–15). Throughout the Bible, the kings of Israel, including the greatest of them, David and Solomon, were never perceived as above the law (II Samuel 12:7–13, I Kings 11:7–12) or as incarnations of the divine, as the Egyptians, Babylonians, and Romans viewed their rulers. The kings of Israel and Judah were, first and foremost, human beings, elevated in rank, but human nonetheless. That the Bible paints a less than flattering overall portrait of Israel's experiences with monarchy simply confirms this understanding. Thus, here too, the idea in the *Protocols* of a "King of the Jews" imposed by Jews on gentiles reflects neither any understanding whatsoever of Jewish attitudes toward kingship nor the reality of the Jews' experience with their monarchs.

Nor do the *Protocols* reflect a realistic assessment of Israelite or Jewish attitudes toward the larger society. From both a biblical and postbiblical Jewish perspective, the responsibilities of society include providing for the educational, judicial, financial, and general welfare needs of those who are its members as well as the defense of its citizenry. All of these responsibilities came under the same rubrics of justice and righteousness. As the prophets of ancient Israel continuously stressed, anything less would be a betrayal of the divine mandate.

Protocol 6

The Acquisition of Land and the Encouragement of Speculation

Outline

- Establishment of monopolies, huge reservoirs of wealth.
- Development of the super-government, which will reward those who subjugate themselves.
- The Gentile as a landowner is "harmful to us" as it means independence in sources of supply.
- Land must come under control by increasing land obligations.
- Then, "land ownership will be on a par with servitude."
- Encouragement of speculation by which "money shall pass into our hands."
- Gentiles will then be thrown into the ranks of the proletariat.
- Raising of wages to give no relief, as prices of necessities will also rise.
- Undermining of the sources of industry by teaching workmen anarchy and the use of alcohol.
- Active propaganda masked by a pretended desire to help working classes.

Arguments

- We shall soon begin to establish huge monopolies, colossal reservoirs of wealth, upon which even the big Gentile properties will be dependent to such an extent that they will all fall, together with the government credit, on the day following the political catastrophe.
- The aristocracy of the Gentiles as a political force has passed away.
- The best means to attain this [i.e., deprive Gentiles of land] is to increase land taxes and mortgage indebtedness.
- At the same time, it is necessary to encourage trade and industry vigorously and especially speculation, the function of which is to act as a counterpoise to industry.
- To destroy Gentile industry, we shall, as an incentive to this

See original *Protocol* page 165.

speculation, encourage among the Gentiles a strong demand for luxuries, all-enticing luxuries.

- We will force up wages, which, however, will be of no benefit to workers, for we will at the same time cause a rise in the prices of prime necessities, pretending that this is due to the decline of agriculture and cattle raising.
- That the true situation shall not be noticed by the Gentiles prematurely, we will mask it by a pretended effort to serve the working classes and promote great economic principles, for which an active propaganda will be carried on through our economic theories.

Refuting Protocol 6

In addition to the supposedly contemptuous attitude of the Jewish people toward non-Jews, the central lie of the sixth protocol is the contempt for non-Jews who own land as well as for the land itself. This is a view totally at odds with what we find in the Scriptures as well with Jewish life as demonstrated throughout postbiblical Jewish thought and history.

First, it is not accidental that throughout the Jewish Scriptures, the Land of Israel, *Eretz Yisrael* in Hebrew, was known as the Holy Land. This is the land where God's covenant with Israel was to be fulfilled, the land where, in their holiest city, Jerusalem, the people of Israel would build their sanctuaries and Temple. Even before its habitation by Israel, it was described as a land of enormous agricultural fertility, "flowing with milk and honey." Nor can one read the literature of the prophets of ancient Israel without realizing that the agricultural life of Israel was the idealized Israelite existence (see, for instance, I Kings 5:5, Amos 9:13–15, Zechariah 3:10, Ezekiel 36:8).

Second, religiously, any number of Jewish festivals and fast days are land-based events: Pesach (Passover), Shavuot (Festival of Pentecost), and the Seven Weeks counting between them; Sukkot (Festival of Tabernacles), and Tu B'Sh'vat (Arbor Day) are all thematically and historically tied directly to the Land of Israel (see Exodus 23:14–17, Deuteronomy 16:1–16).

Third, contemporarily, the rise of modern Zionism at the end of the nineteenth and beginning of the twentieth centuries saw the path to national rebirth and redemption as coming through the revitalization of the land. The only way in which the age-old Jewish dream of a resurrected Jewish commonwealth could be realized would be by reclaiming the land. In practical terms, this meant that Jews, coming primarily from Eastern Europe, worked to clear the rocks, irrigate the sands, and drain the swamps to make the land bloom once again. These earliest modern pioneers, even those without the necessary agricultural or farming experience, knew in the very marrow of their bones that the key to their success was a reborn and revitalized Land of Israel. The early twentieth-century Zionist leader A. D. Gordon helped inspire these pioneers. He wrote: "We must do ourselves all the work, from the least strenuous, cleanest and most sophisticated, to the dirtiest and most difficult" (Gordon, "The Ideal of Labor," cited in Glatzer, *The Dynamics of Emancipation*, p. 177). Today, the State of Israel continues to be one of the most agriculturally advanced and productive in the Middle Eastern region, exporting many of its farm products not only to Europe, but to the United States.

Thus, there is literally nothing in the whole of the Jewish religious and legal tradition, nor in the Bible, which shows anything other than profound respect for the land as a gift from God, including the holiness of the Land of Israel. In Deuteronomy 11:11–12, God tells the Children of Israel that "the land you are about to cross into . . . is a land which the Lord your God looks after, which the Lord your God always keeps His eye on".

Equally, there is nothing in either aspect of Jewish life which evinces contempt for non-Jewish land ownership even in the Land of Israel. Of this last point, one has only to recall Abraham's insistence upon paying Ephron the Hittite for the burial cave at Machpelah for his beloved wife Sarah, and his respectful attitude throughout the negotiations (Genesis 23). Note also how God instructs Abraham to properly acquire the land, so that his descendants can "enter it as heirs, not robbers" (BT Bava Batra 100a, ed. Soncino, p. 418, n. 11).

This attitude toward the Holy Land and its produce is further expressed in the commandment of Deuteronomy 20:18–19, where God tells the Jews not to destroy fruit-bearing trees, even during a time of war. This rejection of "scorched earth" tactics stands as one of the earliest ecological expressions in history. The rabbis widened this commandment to apply to all of nature, not just to the specifics of the verse.

It must be noted, in addition, that fully one sixth of the oldest Jewish law code, the Mishnah, is devoted to laws, both proscriptive and prescriptive, relating to agriculture. Furthermore, Jews always formed agrarian societies until they were no longer allowed to do so by their foreign overlords. For example, the Jewish community in Babylonia of the third to seventh centuries continued to live on the land until the Baghdadian caliphate effected their movement into urban centers. Throughout Jewish history, including medieval France and Provence, Jews engaged in farming, viticulture, and other agricultural pursuits.

Protocol 7

A Prophecy of a Worldwide War

Outline

- As preparatory measures, concentration of armaments and the growth of the police powers of states are necessary.
- Only need is that of the proletarians, a few friendly millionaires, politicians, and soldiers.
- In creating disorder and animosities, fear is inculcated, and governmental cabinets and politics are entangled by cunning and evasiveness.

Arguments

- Increasing concentration of armaments, enlargement of the police powers of the state, these are all essential to the completion of the above-mentioned plans.
- We must create unrest, dissension, and mutual animosities throughout Europe and, with the help of her relationship, on other continents.
- To each act of opposition, we must be in a position to respond by bringing on war with the neighbors of any country that dares to oppose us, and if those neighbors should plan to stand collectively against us, we must let loose a worldwide war.
- The chief element of success in politics lies in the secrecy of undertakings.
- We must force the Gentile governments to adopt measures which will promote our broadly conceived plan, already approaching its triumphant goal, by bringing to bear the pressure of stimulated public opinion, which has in reality been organized by us with the help of the so-called "great power" of the press.
- In a word, to demonstrate our enslavement of the Gentile governments of Europe, we shall show our power to one of them by crimes of violence, that is, by a reign of terror, and if they should permit themselves to rebel against us, we shall answer them all with American, Chinese, or Japanese guns.

See original *Protocol* page 167.

Refuting Protocol 7

The central charge of the seventh protocol is that Jews sow the seeds of internal unrest and discord. This assumption, like so many of the false charges in this work, is the very antithesis of what both ancient Israelites and contemporary Jews regard as the ideal of societal harmony. Indeed, Protocol 7 claims that there is an attempt to create a "spill-over effect" that would lead to war between nations. Such a vision is the very opposite of Israel's historic commitment to the goal of attaining *shalom*, "peace."

Central to Judaism is not only the ritual and ceremonial, but also the moral-ethical. This commitment was translated into both courts of law and administration by magistrates appointed by Moses and, in rabbinic times, to a court system leading up to the Sanhedrin (High Court). In both Exodus and Deuteronomy, Moses appoints others to decide lesser disputes, reserving for himself the more difficult cases. In the biblical books, those designated as judges were to be men of sterling character, without blemish, knowledgeable, above suspicion and corruption, and influenced neither by the very wealthy or the very poor (see Exodus 18 and Deuteronomy 1, as well as the refutation to Protocol 3).

Postbiblically, the rabbis established three kinds of courts: civil courts of three judges, courts of twenty-three judges to deal with capital cases, and the Sanhedrin of seventy-one judges which handled matters of national importance, such as the Temple, and was also the final court of appeal. So seriously do the Jewish people continue to take legal matters and communal harmony that many still look toward a *bet din* (Jewish court) to resolve disputes. In addition, the commitment not only to scholarship, but to the rule of law continues to be reflected in the traditional wording of rabbinical ordination "May he teach? Yes, he may teach. May he adjudicate the law? Yes, he may adjudicate the law" (BT Sanhedrin 5a).

More to the point, Israel's earliest history through the destruction of the Second Temple by the Romans in the year 70 was a history often dominated by war. Its subsequent nearly two-thousand-year dispersion, primarily in the Western world, and up to and including the present day, has also, too often, been a story of wars and violence. Yet, despite this tragedy, throughout the Scriptures and later Jewish literature, the dream and hope of *shalom*, of peace, between the Jewish people and those with whom they come into contact, remains paramount. The summation of this dream can be found in chapter 4:1–5 of the prophet Micah:

> In the days to come,
> The mount of the Lord's House shall stand
> Firm above the mountains,
> And it shall tower above the hills;
> And peoples shall gaze on it with joy.
> And the many nations shall go and shall say:
> "Come,
> Let us go up to the mount of the Lord,
> To the house of the God of Jacob;
> That He may instruct us in His ways,
> And that we may walk in His paths";
> For instruction shall come forth from Zion,
> The word of the Lord from Jerusalem. Thus He will judge
> among the many peoples,
> And arbitrate for the multitude of nations;
> And they shall beat their swords into plowshares,
> And their spears into pruning hooks;
> Nation shall not take up sword against nation,
> They shall never again know war.
> But every man shall sit under
> his grapevine or fig tree;
> With no one to disturb him.
> For it was the Lord of hosts who spoke.
> Though all the peoples walk each in the name of its gods,
> We will walk
> In the name of the Lord our God forever and ever.

Such magnificent sentiments echo throughout Scripture (Psalms, Ecclesiastes, Job, Kings, and, of course, Isaiah). Then, too, there is the last line of the Priestly Benediction, still in use today, from the Book of Numbers (6:26): "May God lift your face to His and give you peace."

Later Jewish literature, too, through its commentaries emphasized the hope for *shalom*. In the rabbinic collection of ethical maxims known as the *Ethics of the Fathers*, this statement is attributed to the first-century Rabbinic leader Simeon the son of Gamaliel: "By three things is the world sustained: By justice, by truth and by peace" (*Ethics of the Fathers* 1:18, in Goldin, *The Living Talmud*, p. 75). Indeed, the rabbis write that Shalom is one of the many names for God ("here the [Holy] Name itself is designated 'Peace' [Shalom]," BT Shabbat 10a, Soncino p. 37). This is indicative of the very essence of the divine nature, and therefore also implanted in the human soul.

The Mishnah tells us that in the Rabbinic view, peace was seen as an ultimate blessing: "R. Simeon b. Halafta said: The Holy One, blessed is he, found no vessel that could hold Israel's blessing excepting peace, for it is written, 'The Lord will give strength to his people; the Lord will bless people in peace' " (Mishnah Uktzin 3:12, Danby, p. 789). Even the prayer that is recited by mourners, which reminds us of the glory and power of God, concludes with the line: "May He who makes peace in the heavens make peace on earth. Amen."

But peace was not only something to be received passively; Jews were in fact commanded to actively pursue it (Leviticus Rabbah 9:9). The force of this teaching was so powerful, and was absorbed by so many generations of Jews, that in the eighteenth century, a Lithuanian Jew would declare to his descendants in his will "To be at peace with all this world, with Jew and Gentile, must be your foremost aim in this terrestrial life. . . . For the main thing is peace, peace with the whole world" (Joel ben Abraham Shemariah, cited in Glatzer, *Faith and Knowledge*, pp. 106–107).

Finally, a modern Israeli thinker, Aviezer Ravitzky, sums up the Jewish concept of peace. "The Hebrew word for peace, shalom, is derived from a root denoting wholeness or completeness, and its frame of reference throughout Jewish literature is bound up with the notion of shlemut, perfection" (in A. Cohen and P. Mendes-Flohr, *Contemporary Jewish Religious Thought*, p. 685).

The pursuit of an ideal of peace is exactly the opposite of the claim of the seventh protocol. Thus, the premises upon which this protocol is based are, again, false in their assumptions and a denial of both the Jewish Scriptures and the Jewish ethical tradition.

Protocol 8

The Transitional Government

Outline

- "Subtle expressions and evasions" will justify unjust laws.
- The government will be surrounded by specialists who know the secrets of social existence, hidden meanings in politics, and who are familiar with the seamy side of human nature.
- Gentiles will not be recruited for this work.
- Economists who are chiefly Jews will swarm.
- Everything, in the last analysis, will be decided by figures.
- Only Gentiles "with a past" will be trusted.

Arguments

- We must provide ourselves with the same weapons which our enemies might employ against us.
- Our government will surround itself with all the forces of the civilization in the midst of which it is to function.
- Such persons will comprehend all the secrets of social being.
- We will surround our government with a whole world of economists.
- For the time being, until it is safe to give responsible government positions to our brother Jews, we shall entrust them to people whose past and whose character are such that there is an abyss between them and the people; to people for whom, in case of disobedience of our orders, there will remain only the alternative of trial or exile, thus forcing them to protect our interests to their last breath.

Refuting Protocol 8

The false assumptions of the eighth protocol are two: first, the alleged economic exploitation of non-Jews based upon a jaundiced view of Jewish business and commerce—this charge was refuted above in *Protocols* 2 and 4; and second, the equally invalid claim that Jews exploit the so-called criminal element of

See original *Protocol* page 168.

society for their own benefit. Nothing could be further from the truth! As the *Encyclopaedia Judaica* correctly notes: "Jews in the Diaspora have generally been less involved in crime than populations among which they have lived. Their closely knit communities, cohesive family life, high educational standards, moderation in the consumption of alcohol, their solidarity, consciousness of mutual responsibility, and readiness for mutual help, are regarded as the main causes for the generally low crime rates among Jews"(s.v. "Crime," vol. 5, cols. 1091–1103).

The article, additionally, makes the following important points: "In the first place, Jewish crime rates were lowest where Jews were discriminated against and actually increased after Emancipation. Second, crimes committed by Jewish offenders were generally different in character in countries of discrimination and persecution from those committed by members of the dominant population groups. The more the Jews became emancipated and were enabled to participate in social, economic, and cultural life, the crimes committed by them became more similar to those of the majority population."

This is not to imply that Jews historically and at present have not had among them people who committed crimes. It is to say, however, that such instances were fewer than in the dominant or larger population in any country where such statistics have been kept precisely, and this was so because of the characteristic values enumerated above: emphasis on education, importance of family life, cohesiveness of communal life, sense of responsibility to and for the community, and lower rates of alcohol (and drug) consumption. If one did sin or commit a crime, and honestly repented (true repentance involves not just verbal apologies, but also direct action that demonstrates the sincerity of the repentance), then the past deeds are not to be held against such a person, and he or she is considered healed and fully reintegrated into communal life.

Thus, conjuring up the image of villainous Jewish leaders exploiting the so-called criminal element is wholly without substance. Further, it is a charge that stands in stark opposition to the values reflected in the fact that far fewer Jews commit crimes than the members of any of the larger host populations among whom Jews have lived.

Protocol 9

The All-Embracing Propaganda

Outline

- "In advancing our plans, take notice of the character of the people in whose countries you are resident."
- "Liberty, Equality, Fraternity.
- Antisemitism has its place in restraining the Jewish proletariat.
- The super-government is to be a dictatorship.
- Monarchists, demagogues, socialists, communists, and utopians generally are "all in our service," all undermining authority and the existing order.
- The masses demand solution of social problems by international agreement.
- Coalition between rulers and masses is not to the advantage of the Jews.
- False economic theories and principles stimulated by us.
- Forestalling armed uprising.

Arguments

- In applying our principles, give attention to the character of the people of those countries in which you will reside and work.
- For the words of the liberal slogan, actually those of our Masonic passwords, "Liberty, Equality, Fraternity," when we reign we will substitute a modification in the words, "The right of Liberty, the duty of Equality, the ideal of Fraternity."
- In reality there are no obstacles for us.
- From us emanates a far-reaching terror.
- The masses are clamoring concerning the necessity of solving social problems by means of international agreement.
- We might fear the combined strength of the Gentiles of vision with the blind power of the masses, but we have taken all measures against such a possible contingency by raising a wall of mutual antagonism between these two forces.
- In order that the hand of the blind masses may not free itself

See original *Protocol* page 170.

from the grasp of our leadership, we must at all times be in close touch with them; if not personally, then through our most trusted brethren.

- How to verify that which is taught in the village schools?
- In order not to prematurely destroy the Gentile institutions, we have laid our efficient hands on them, and grasped the springs of their mechanism.
- We have misled, stupefied, and demoralized the youth of the Gentiles by means of education in principles and theories, patently false to us but which we have inspired.
- Above existing laws, without actual change but by distorting them through contradictory interpretations, we have created something stupendous in the way of results.
- You say that they will rise in arms against us if they discover the true state of affairs before the time is ripe. *In anticipation of this, we have prepared in the West a maneuver so terrifying that the bravest souls will shudder. Underground railways and passages will be established by that time in all capitals, and they will be blown up, together with all their institutions and public records.**

Refuting Protocol 9

The ninth protocol falsely ascribes to Jews what is the antithesis of Jewish belief and the Jewish historical experience in three specific areas: (1) law, (2) education, and (3) Masonry and Freemasonry.

Let us take each charge in turn.

Throughout the *Protocols*, the author, or authors, attributes to the Jewish people a thorough-going disrespect for law as the stabilizing element in society and the use of violence to achieve so-called Jewish ends. The idea of a plot organized by Jews to set off a violent act of detonation, so as to achieve massive destruction and wanton murder in the capital cities of Europe, and, thereby, introduce chaos into society, is totally a fictional creation of those who wrote this text. Such plots or actions have no

---

*Emphasis in original text.

basis whatsoever in any source or literature of the Jewish people. Furthermore, the absurdity of the charge can be seen in the fact that in the last century, no explosion of that sort, nor any store of explosives in those areas, was ever recorded.

Indeed, what marked biblical Israel's unique understanding of law as the basis of individual and societal morality was the view that law stemmed directly from God, and thus its authority and sanctity were above reproach. This unique understanding was epitomized by the prophets of ancient Israel, who, when directly addressing the corruption of the day, called upon Israel to repent, by invoking Divine wrath where appropriate, and by emphasizing that these demands were to be reinforced by the force of law.

The talmudic ruling *dina de-malchuta dina* ("the law of the country [or, government] is law") (BT Nedarim 28a, ed. Soncino, p. 80, Gittin 10b, Soncino p. 37) has been upheld ever since medieval times. This law states simply that Jews are required to follow the laws of the countries in which they live. Thus, for example, according to Jewish law, it is forbidden to evade taxes or file a dishonest tax return.

Postbiblically, throughout the rabbinic period up to and including the modern era, the interweaving of law and morality has continued, with two further insights: (1) the purpose of moral behavior and law is to ensure peace throughout society, and (2) such behavior, having the force of law, is of direct benefit to society, energizing it to further its positive accomplishments and overcome its deficiencies. And, as noted previously in the discussion of the fifth protocol, Israel's religious development was a mixing of ritual and ethics, ceremonies and morality. Thus, any description of the Jewish approach to law and morality that fails to present these ancient fundamentals, along with their current validity, is totally false.

Equally important is the Jewish belief in the importance of education in the life of the individual, the Jewish community, and the greater general community and society. For example, the Book of Deuteronomy (6:20 ff.) reminds the Israelites to teach their children how God forged a nation by taking it from slavery to freedom. Such instruction, throughout the Scriptures, was keyed to the goal of producing a "kingdom of priests and a holy people," as noted in Exodus. Thus, Israel and the Jewish people continue to affirm that "awe of God is the foundation of wisdom [i.e., knowledge]," as recorded in Psalms 111:10 and Proverbs 1:7. The Book of Proverbs is best understood as a curriculum guidebook for the spiritual, moral, and character education of those who would one day aspire to leadership.

The value of education was not limited to the study of religious and ethical concepts. The reward of work, as expressed in Psalms 128:1–2, "Happy are all who fear the Lord, who follow his ways. You shall enjoy the fruit of your labors, you shall be happy and you shall prosper," meant that practical education was also required. The Talmud (BT Kiddushin 82a–b, ed. Soncino, pp. 424–425) has an extensive discussion on what crafts are best for a father to teach his son. Elsewhere (BT Pesahim 113a, ed. Soncino, p. 580), a talmudic master tells his disciple: "Deal in carcasses but do not deal in words, flay carcasses in the marketplace and earn wages and do not say, 'I am a priest and a great man, and it is beneath my dignity.'" Furthermore, the Talmud ruled that one who is not employed in work that is "concerned with the general welfare" of humanity is not eligible to be accepted as a witness (Sanhedrin 24b, ed. Soncino, p. 143). In the medieval period, Maimonides vehemently stressed the importance of work for all, even scholars: "One, however, who makes up his mind to study Torah and not work but live on charity, profanes the name of God, brings the Torah into contempt, extinguishes the light of religion, brings evil upon himself, and deprives himself of life in the world to come. . . . It indicates a high degree of excellence in a man to maintain himself by the labor of his hands" (*Mishneh Torah*, Hilchot Talmud Torah 6:13, cited in Glatzer, *Faith and Knowledge*, p. 70).

Further, the very word *torah* which designates the entire collection of biblical books, while more often than not mistranslated as "law," really means "teaching." For, in truth, that was and is what the Bible has meant to the Jewish people throughout time. It is a book of teachings designed to foster holy living by its synthesis of ritual and ethical, ceremonial and moral norms. Thus, throughout the various biblical books, the word *torah* appears not as reference to the written text, but as the citing of individual teachings which the reader/hearer should personally take to heart and apply in everyday life.

Furthermore, the Torah in the larger sense, encompassing Genesis through Deuteronomy and also, in a wider sense, Genesis through Second Chronicles, is a written text of the core teachings of the Jewish people. As a result, Jewish education from generation to generation has been text-based and requires of its adherents knowledge of both the alphabet and the ability to read. Therefore, literacy and the ability both to analyze and interpret the holy words of the text have always been, and remain to this day, hallmarks of Jewish education.

Thus the perversion of the educational process alleged in this protocol for political, economic, or socially manipulative ends is, like the perversion of the Jewish legal process discussed above, in total opposition to the Jewish understanding and commitment to these basic societal foundations.

Lastly, the supreme historical irony of this and subsequent protocols is the attribution of Masonry/Freemasonry as part of some secretive Jewish cabal. The protocol pretends to trace its origins to the builders of Solomon's Temple, (ca. 964 B.C.E.), who were mainly Israelites. In truth, this fraternal society was founded in the seventeenth century in England and spread throughout Europe, especially Germany and France, and later to both the United States and the Middle East.

What is omitted from the *Protocols* is the fact that the Freemasons have excluded and continue to exclude Jews from much of their worldwide membership. The Masons perceive themselves as a Christian, though not a Catholic, organization. Only in modern times has Masonic practice opened its doors to Jewish membership in the United States and in Israel.

The closed ritual practices of Freemasonry, based upon its own reinterpretation of Scriptures, lent themselves quite naturally to those who fostered the *Protocols* and falsely perceived the Masonic Order as being under the supposed leadership of the non-existent "Learned Elders of Zion." However, there is not and never was any organizational relationship whatsoever between Judaism, the Jewish people, and the Masonic Order. In addition, while there are now a number of Masonic lodges whose membership is predominately composed of Jews, the Masons' fraternal and social agenda is of their own devising and has no connection whatsoever with Judaism.

Protocol 10

Abolition of the Constitution; Rise of the Autocracy

Outline

- The masses are satisfied by visible results in politics, and to them nothing is more important than pleasure.
- No serious problems can be presented to the masses.
- Consequently, there is freedom of political action for us in reticence.
- The vote to disappear.
- Absolutism of the majority not to be obtained from the intellectual classes.
- Individualism to pass.
- Jewish blind authority to replace Gentile leaders.
- Democracy in government planning leads to kaleidoscopic misconceptions.
- Organization of contemporary institutions to be changed and harmonized with our plans.
- Introduction of the poison of liberalism causes a fatal weakness.
- Constitutionalism is only a school for dispute, disagreement, and party agitation.
- A president and officials with "Panamas."
- The Chamber of Deputies to be deprived of all powers.
- Presidential authority to be attacked.
- He will turn to the masses, the leaders of which "we" control.
- "Political secrets must be preserved" as an excuse for withholding information.
- Hostile legislative activity to be curbed by an appeal to the international majority.
- Shortening parliamentary sessions.
- Stirring up trouble in the official family.
- Destruction and imperceptible abolition of constitutions melting the government into an autocracy.

See original *Protocol* page 173.

Arguments

- Today I shall begin by repeating what has already been stated. I beg you to remember that politics, governments and the masses are satisfied with appearances.
- The people feel an especial love and respect toward the genius who wields political power, and they say of all his high-handed actions: "It is base but clever! It is a trick, but how he played it! So majestic! So impudent!"
- When we accomplish our government *coup d'état*, we will say to the people: "Everything has gone badly, all have suffered. We will eliminate the causes of your sufferings—nationality, frontiers, and diversity of coinage. Of course, you are free to pronounce sentence upon us, but that can scarcely be just if you do so before giving a trial to that which we offer you."
- To this end we must introduce universal suffrage without distinction of class or caste, so as to establish the absolutism of the majority which cannot be obtained by a vote of the intellectual classes or of castes.
- Having in this way inspired everybody with the thought of their own importance, we will break down the influence of family life among the Gentiles and its educational importance.
- The scheme of administration must emanate from a single brain, for it cannot be established if we allow it to be divided into disconnected segments through the work of many minds.
- Our plans will not upset contemporary institutions immediately.
- Approximately the same institutions exist in different countries under different names: representatives, ministries, senates, state councils, legislative and executive bodies.
- When we introduced the poison of liberalism into the governmental organism, its entire political complexion changed.
- Constitutional governments were born of liberalism, replacing the autocracy that was the salvation of the Gentiles.
- In the near future, we shall establish the responsibility of presidents.
- In order to achieve this result, we will manipulate the election of presidents whose past contains some undisclosed dark affair, some "Panamas."*

*This refers to alleged financial misdealing in the construction of the Panama Canal.

- It is obvious that under these circumstances the key to the shrine will be in our hands and that no one but ourselves will guide the legislative power.
- Besides this, with the introduction of the new constitution of the republic, we will take away from the Chamber the right of interpellations concerning government measures, under the pretext of guarding political secrets.
- Upon the president will depend the naming of the presidents and vice-presidents of the Chamber.
- The president, under our direction, will interpret in various ways the meaning of such existing laws as can be differently interpreted.
- These measures will give us the possibility of eliminating, little by little and step by step, all that which we may be obliged, at the beginning, to introduce into the government constitution, in the endeavor to acquire our rights, so as to bring about, unobserved, the abolition of every constitution and, when the time comes, to merge every function into our autocracy.
- The recognition of our autocrat may come even before the abolition of the constitution.
- But you well know that to make possible the universal expression of such a desire, it is necessary incessantly to disturb the relations between peoples and governments in all countries, so as to wear everyone out by dissensions, animosities, feuds, even martyrdom, famine, inoculation of diseases, want, until the Gentiles see no other escape except an appeal to our money and power and for our supreme rule.
- Should we give the people a breathing space, however, the desired moment may never come.

Refuting Protocol 10

Once again, in the tenth protocol, we see the perversion of Jewish values wherein an alleged contempt for the political process on the part of Jews is paraded. This protocol claims that Jews prefer autocratic, authoritarian rule to representative and participatory forms of government coupled with disrespect for constitutional rule. It also alleges that Jews lack respect for involvement in the life of the community and/or nation-state, and also do not respect family life (especially the non-Jewish family).

As with the previous libels in the *Protocols*, these assertions are absolutely without any merit or basis in history. Beginning primarily with the emancipation of Jews in Europe and the United States at the end of the eighteenth century, Jews have actively involved themselves in the political life of their world. Moreover, while particular Jewish concerns have always been part of the overall agenda, Jewish ethics of political involvement has mandated a concern for the greater whole and the greater good.

Thus, for example, built into the Jewish legal system is the understanding that decisions passed by majority rule are communally enforceable and binding upon both majority and minority. Equally significant is the Jewish affirmation of the principle expressed in *dina de malchuta dina* ("the law of the kingdom is the law,") already discussed above in regard to Protocol 9), by which Jews understand their responsibility to be law-abiding citizens of their country of residence. Although the type of rule during the biblical period was mostly a monarchy, it was never meant to be absolute or totalitarian. The approval of the Sanhedrin, or High Court, was required for any declaration of war (JT Sanhedrin 1).

Furthermore, the contempt Jews are said to have for constitutional and representative forms of government is equally false. To be historically accurate, since the eighteenth century, Jews generally have fared better and involved themselves more in political activities where both the governments and economic systems were liberal, that is, open and not hostile to competing points of view, with respect and toleration for all. Then, too, as noted previously in Protocol 9, the Jewish religious tradition and heritage, with its text-based religious tradition committed to law as the foundation of society, is, by definition, a system which values the ideals of constitutional government. Authoritarian autocratic rule by which one individual or a select group of self-designated leaders arrogate to themselves the leadership of any society or nation-state, and who claim to know what is in the best interests of society as a whole, is an idea that is the very opposite of Jewish mores.

One of the great strengths of the Jewish people, demonstrated through the centuries, is its emphasis on the family rather than the individual as the basic building block of society, and, by extension, its understanding of community and society as an ever larger family.

From the biblical period on, the focus has been on husbands and wives, parents and children, sons and daughters, brothers and sisters. Marriage is considered the ideal state of relationship with which to serve God; children the blessing which completes the picture and makes the family unit whole. According to the Midrash: "He who has no wife dwells without good, without help, without joy, without blessing and without atonement" (Genesis Rabbah, 17:22, ed. Soncino, p.132). Non-Jews were seen in this context as having the same responsibility to marry and have children. It is worth noting that when the rabbis were asked to give an example of honoring parents, the example used was that of a Gentile (Deuteronomy Rabbah, 1:15, ed. Soncino, p. 16). Basic familial and societal responsibilities incumbent upon the Jewish people were summarized for non-Jews in the seven Noahide laws, which applied to society as a whole: to create courts of justice; to condemn and punish crimes of idolatry, blasphemy, incest, murder, and robbery, and to refrain from eating the limb of a living animal (BT Sanhedrin 56a, ed. Soncino, pp. 381–382).

Thus, the alleged contempt of Jews for involvement in the political process, their supposed rejection of respect and toleration for others with differing political perspectives, and their alleged disdain for everything understood by the term "family" are the very antithesis of what Judaism stands for and what Jews have been taught down through the centuries.

Protocol 11

The Constitution of Autocracy and Universal Rule

Outline

- The new constitution which establishes the government council as the visible part of the legislative body.
- Law, the judiciary, and the court followed by *coup d'état*.
- Freedom of expression to be silenced on appearance of the new constitution.
- Care in the promulgation of new ordinances.
- Despair following strictness and leniency are both detrimental to the new constitution.
- Quick action following terror and surprise of revolution fixes authority.
- Promises not to be kept.
- The threshold of universal rule.

Arguments

- The Council of State will accentuate the authority of the ruler.
- The following is a complete resume of the new constitution now in preparation. We will create a law-code, jurisprudence, and courts:
  1. In the form of recommendations to the legislative body.
  2. By Presidential decrees in the form of general statutes, by Senate ordinances and by decisions of the Council of State in the form of ministerial ordinances.
  3. In case the opportune moment arrives, through a *coup d'état*, overturning the government.
- Having outlined approximately the *modus agendi*, we will now take up in detail those combinations by means of which we will finally reverse the movement of the government machinery and cause it to turn in the direction herein before mentioned.
- It is essential for us that from the first moment of its promulgation, while the people are still dumbfounded by the *coup d'état* and in a state of terror and indecision, they should realize that

See original *Protocol* page 180.

we are so powerful and so unassailable that we will under no
condition give them any consideration, and that not only will
we ignore their opinions and wishes but that we are ready and
able to suppress, with overwhelming authority, their manifestations and demonstrations at every time and place; that we
have seized outright everything we wanted, and that we will
not divide our power with them under any circumstances.
- The Gentiles are like a flock of sheep and we are to them as
wolves.
- They will close their eyes to everything because we will promise to return all the liberties taken away, after the enemies of
peace have been subjugated and all parties pacified.
- For what have we conceived all this program and instilled its
measures into the minds of the Gentiles without giving them
the possiblity of examining its underside, if it is not for the
purpose of attaining by circuitous methods that which is at-
tainable to our scattered race by a direct route?
- This has served as a foundation for our organization of secret
Masonry. The aims of which are unknown and are not even
suspected by the Gentile cattle, attracted by us into the visible
army of the Masonic Lodges, so as to detract the attention of
their compatriots.
- God gave to us, His Chosen People, as a blessing, the dispersal,
and this which has appeared to all to be our weakness has
been our whole strength.
- Little remains to be built on these foundations.

Refuting Protocol 11

Having already addressed two of the main issues with which
this protocol is concerned, the supposed anti-Gentile orientation
of the Jewish people and Judaism and the false understanding
and misinterpretation of Scripture's idea of Israel as the Chosen
People (which were refuted in the responses to *Protocols* 3, 4, 5,
and 6), there remains little to be said but to restate the obvious
about these two indictments: first, that the enemies of the Jewish
people, who falsely accuse Jews of harboring diabolical attitudes, hate, and arrogance, themselves display these very atti-

tudes toward Jews and Judaism; and second, that to be chosen by God, at least according to the Hebrew Bible, means to be selected for greater responsibility, that is, to be a "living witness" to the Presence of God in the midst of humanity, and, in the process, to run the risk of a greater punishment for the failure to do so. It in no way implies or confers superiority on those so selected or inferiority on those not selected.

Also previously addressed was the Israelite-Jewish understanding of Jewish participation in the larger society and the political process, especially in the refutations of *Protocols* 3, 5, 7, 9, and 10. Once again, Jewish sources and experiences are the opposite of what is presented in this protocol. Contrary to what is written here, Jewish involvement in the life of the host community is *not* intended to foment revolution, political unrest, and societal chaos, but, rather, to produce committed citizens, who are willing to work for society's betterment through all appropriate channels. Further, a Jew should always be governed by the highest moral and ethical considerations as expressed in the Jewish religious tradition.

The other so-called issue presented in this protocol and already addressed in the refutation of the ninth is that of Masonry. As already stated, it is absolutely absurd (and antisemitic) to attribute to Jews manipulative power over an organization founded in the seventeenth century by Christians. The original United Grand Lodge was founded in London, England, in 1717, uniting four lodges in that city and country. Subsequently, members in other countries formed their own Grand Lodges. A difference in thinking led other lodges in England to form their own Grand Lodge, but the two were united in 1813. In 1725, in Paris, an Englishman formed the Grand Orient Lodge, which eventually united with the English Grand Lodge in 1773. Jews played no part whatsoever in any of this. Additionally, the *Book of Constitutions*, which spells out the history, rituals, and structure of the English Masonic organization was written in 1722–23 by the Reverend James Anderson of the Church of Scotland at the request of the Grand Lodge of London. Again, no Jews were involved.

Protocol 12

The Kingdom of the Press and its Control

Outline

- A definition of "Liberty," a word which will mean what we will.
- Tight rein upon the press.
- Pamphleteering to be made costly.
- Special stamp taxes on publications.
- Press espionage and methods of supervision.
- Heavy fines for those who attack.
- Suppression.
- Control of the worldwide news agencies.
- All liberals are anarchistic in thought.
- Protest for the sake of protest.
- The absolute control of cheap publications.
- Licenses to publish.
- Government ownership of newspapers.
- Conflicting propaganda to confuse readers and show an apparent division of opinion.
- Official organs and those designed to attract the indifferent.
- Periodicals of apparent opposition used to disclose enemies and to superficially oppose non-essentials.
- Press freedom to be apparent only.
- Dreams of the provincials.
- Aligning the country against the city.
- Social dishonesty and crime not to be exposed.

Arguments

- The word "Liberty," which may be variously interpreted, we will define as follows:
- Liberty is the right to do that which is permitted by law.
- Such a definition will eventually serve us, because all limitations of liberty obviously will be in our hands, for the laws will either permit or forbid only that which we wish, in accordance with the foregoing program.

See original *Protocol* page 182.

- We shall handle the press in the following manner:
- Not one announcement will reach the people save under our supervision.
- If we have already managed to dominate the mind of Gentile society to such a point that almost all see world affairs through the colored lenses of the spectacles which we place before their eyes, and if not, there is not one government with barriers erected against our access to that which by Gentile stupidity is termed state secrets, what then will it be when we are the recognized masters of the world in the person of our universal ruler?
- Let us return to the future of the press. *Everyone desiring to become an editor, librarian, or typographer will be obliged to obtain a license, which in case of offense will be immediately revoked.**
- With such measurers, the handling of thought will be the means of education in the hands of our government, which will not allow the people to be enticed into the pitfalls and dreams of the blessings of progress.
- Let us pass again to the press. *We shall exact stamp taxes per page, and require surety bonds on printed matter and on books of less than thirty pages, a double tax.**
- Literature and journalism are two most important educational forces and consequently our government will become the owner of most of the journals.
- The leading place will be held by organs of an official character.
- Second will be the semiofficial organs, whose point it will be to attract the tepid and indifferent.
- In the third category, we shall place the organs of apparent opposition.
- All our papers will support the most diverse opinions: aristocratic, republican, even anarchistic, so long, of course, as the constitution lives.
- To direct our newspaper militia along this line, we must organize this business with great care.
- These attacks against us will also convince the people of the full freedom of the press, and it will give our agents the oppor-

*Emphasis in original text.

tunity of declaring that the papers opposing us are mere wind-bags, since they cannot find any real arguments to oppose our orders.

- Such measures, positive but imperceptible to the public, will lead public opinion always with increasing success to indicate a trust in our government.
- Already there exists formally in French journalism a tacit ma-sonic solidarity.
- Our calculations reach out especially into the country districts.
- When we enter the period of the new regime, passing over the transition of our accession to power, we must not permit the press to make any exposures of public dishonesty.

Refuting Protocol 12

The twelfth protocol is a continued repetition of the same antise-mitic charges. The so-called issue of constraints upon liberty and freedom, and the denial of this great biblical principle, has al-ready been addressed in the refutation of Protocol 1. The "is-sues" of the journalistic press and censorship were addressed in the refutation of Protocol 2.

What has not yet been addressed is the Jewish attitude toward publishing and literature. Protocol 12 paints a picture of the ma-nipulative use of the written word. In fact, this is the very oppo-site of the Jewish historical experience.

The Bible is the best place to begin any examination of Jewish attitudes toward the written word. The Holy Bible is a written text, and, thus, from earliest times, literacy was required for Is-raelites and their descendants. For how else could the Holy Words of God be pored and reflected over, studied and acted upon? Generation after generation of Jews spent long hours en-gaged in its study (and continue to do so), eliciting every possi-ble meaning, every nuance, every shade of understanding from each book, each chapter, each verse, each word.

Early on, in the postbiblical or Rabbinic period, the tradition of written commentaries to the scriptures arose. These insights were themselves copied and recopied over time. Prior to the in-vention of the printing press, specially trained Jewish scholars called *soferim*, or "scribes," laboriously copied not only the scriptures but also the Talmud and the commentaries as an act of religious and communal commitment and love—a practice still observed among Jews today. Indeed in order to assure an absolutely accurate text, the Talmud [BT Megillah 18b, ed. Soncino, p. 114] ruled that all texts must be copied from another text and not written by memory.

For better than a thousand years, these important works of the Jewish religious tradition were the basic curricula of Jewish religious education. They gave rise to a whole host of corollary literatures based originally on the Scriptures: collections of ethical maxims, interpreted and expanded stories about the principal characters, expanded legal codes based upon Scripture, and the like. Respect for the written word thus became a fundamental Jewish value, literacy the norm, and knowledge the goal and the guide.

In a famous ethical will dating from the twelfth century, a scholarly father wrote to his son: "I have assisted you by providing an extensive library for your use." But the true expression of the Jewish attitude toward the written text came later in the will, where the father commanded his son: "Never refuse to lend books to anyone who has not the means to purchase books for himself" (Judah ibn Tibbon, cited in Glatzer, *Faith and Knowledge*, pp. 72, 76). Here we see that books are not a commodity to be hoarded or collected, but were to be used and shared.

With the invention of the printing press, Jews experienced a literal explosion in the availability of religious texts that has continued uninterruptedly until this day. The accessibility of the written word gave rise to various other types of literature: drama, short stories, novels and novellas, poetry, serious and light nonfiction. For Jews, the Hebrew language has its own holiness ("Just as it [the Torah] was given in the Holy Tongue, so was the world created with the Holy Tongue," Genesis Rabbah 18:4, ed. Soncino, p. 143).

Despite the two-thousand-year exile, Jews maintained their link to the sacred language of Hebrew through their undying commitment to the written word of the holy texts. A sixteenth-century mystic, Rabbi Moses Cordovero, commanded his followers: "Speak Hebrew with your fellows at all times," while a twentieth-century philosopher, Franz Rosenzweig, described

Hebrew as "not the growth of an organism, but the accumulation of a treasury" (cited in Louis Glinert, "Hebrew," Arthur Cohen and Paul Mendes-Flohr, *Contemporary Jewish Religious Thought*, pp. 329–330).

The relationship to Hebrew has been revitalized with the return to Zion and the emergence of the modern State of Israel. Hebrew, the sacred language of the Israelites and later Jews, has reemerged as a living language with a flourishing literature that now shares the spotlight with all of the languages where Jews now dwell throughout the world. Throughout the long march of Jewish history, the written word has been venerated and revered wherever Jews have lived.

Protocol 13

Turning Public Thought from Essentials to Non-essentials

Outline

- Partial starvation as an aid to subjugation.
- Passing laws under cover of contradictory confusion.
- Directing public opinion by a subservient press.
- The raising of unessential political questions.
- Gentile interests turned to trade, pastimes and "people's palaces."
- Losing the power of independent thought.
- Turning Gentile thoughts into lines of progress.
- God's Chosen People are the guardians of truth, and progress is a false conception.
- A plan which is centuries old.

Arguments

- The need of daily bread will force the Gentiles to be silent and make them our obedient servants.
- Then brainless guides of destiny, who even now cannot realize that they do not grasp at all that which they undertake to study, will plunge into the discussion of these new questions.
- From all this you must realize that by getting hold of the opinion of the crowd we only facilitate the functioning of our machinery, and you may also notice that we seek approval, not for our acts, but for our words uttered in regard to one or another question.
- To divert over-restless people from discussing political questions, we shall now bring forward new problems apparently connected with them—problems of industry.
- To prevent them from really thinking out anything themselves we shall deflect their attention to amusements, games, pastimes, excitements, and people's palaces.
- The role of the liberal utopians will be completely played out when our government is recognized.
- When our kingdom is established, our orators will declaim on

See original *Protocol* page 188.

the great problems which have kept humanity in a turmoil to the end that it might finally be brought under our beneficent rule.

Refuting Protocol 13

Back in antiquity, the author of the Book of Ecclesiastes wrote that "there is nothing new under the sun" (1:10). The thirteenth protocol bears witness to this truth. Repetitive lies and false allegations take the place of any serious analysis. In content and style, the *Protocols* were an inspiration and precedent for Nazi Minister of Culture Josef Goebbels, who, during the course of the Third Reich, proclaimed that a lie repeated long enough and loud enough will eventually be believed.

The supposedly contemptuous attitude of Jews toward Gentiles has already been refuted in the response to Protocol 4. Here, the only additional absurdity seems to be the supposed ease with which Gentiles surrender their free thought and independence of action in exchange for the "mindless pleasures" allegedly controlled by Jews. Other themes that are repeated here are the false understanding of Judaism's attitude toward business (Protocol 4), the perverted interpretation of the biblical concepts of chosenness and election (Protocol 3), issues relating to the press and censorship (Protocol 12), and liberalism (Protocol 10).

Perhaps the true intent of the author(s) of the *Protocols* was to provide some kind of summary of the charges which have thus far been hurled against the Jewish people and Judaism. Having done so, he or they now move on. Having already refuted each of them, we are also prepared to move on.

Protocol 14

The Destruction of Religion as a Prelude to the Rise of the Jewish God

Outline

- To destroy all religion as a preparation for the domination of the Jewish God is to be the present aim.
- The teachings of the religion of Moses.
- Gentile mistakes to be portrayed in darkest colors.
- Exploitation of liberty by a mass of adventurers.
- Present social structure to be represented as decayed and of an old type.
- Shortcomings of the Gentile religion.
- The creation of an immoral literature.

Arguments

- When we become rulers, we shall regard as undesirable the existence of any religion except our own, proclaiming one God with Whom our fate is tied as the Chosen People, and by Whom our fate has been made one with the fate of the world.
- On every occasion we will publish articles in which we will compare our beneficent rule with the past.
- The chief strength of our principles and measures will lie in that they are put forward and interpreted by us as a sharp contrast to the old and decayed order of society.
- Our philosophers will discuss all the shortcomings of the Gentile religions, but no one will be allowed to discuss our religion from the true point of view except our own people.
- In countries that are called advanced, we have created a senseless, filthy, and disgusting literature.

Refuting Protocol 14

Religious and theological absurdities abound in the fourteenth protocol. Reference to the "Jewish God" as somehow different from the One God worshipped and venerated by generations

See original *Protocol* page 190.

of Christian faithful is spiritually, theologically, and historically false. Equally false are the references to the "religion of Moses" as somehow other than the foundation upon which Catholic and Protestant Christianity are built. Not surprising is the failure of the *Protocols* to acknowledge that it was within the Jewish community that Jesus was born and spiritually nourished. Such an omission confirms the historical, theological, spiritual, and intellectual dishonesty of the author(s) of the *Protocols*. And lastly, to charge the Jewish people with the creation of a pornographic literature in keeping with its alleged conspiratorial aims is an unsubstantiated charge that can only be explained by antisemitism of the worst kind.

First, the "God of Israel" is worshipped, venerated, adored, and revered by both Judaism and Christianity. There is no accepted Christian religious tradition, whether Catholic, Orthodox, or Protestant, which denies the sacred nature of what Christians call the "Old Testament" and the understanding of God contained within it: that God is One, Holy, Pure, Just, Compassionate, Loving, Lawgiver, Merciful, Incomparable, Creator, and involved not only with the people of Israel (the Jewish people), but with all of humanity. Indeed, according to Christian affirmation, the God of the Gospel of John 3:16 "who so loved the world that He sent His only begotten Son" is the same God! How absurd, then, to write of the "Jewish God" as if that God were somehow other than the One True God of all humanity!

Equally absurd, and obviously directed to the naive and unaware, is the labeling of the "religion of Moses," Judaism, as a sham religion. Does not this charge also denigrate the religion practiced by Jesus and disparage much of what is sacred to Christians?

The beliefs of the "religion of Moses," Judaism, were summarized already in the twelfth century by Moses Maimonides in what has come to be called his "Thirteen Principles of Faith":

(1) Belief in the existence of God
(2) Belief in God's unity
(3) Belief that God is incorporeal (i.e. without form)
(4) Belief that God is eternal
(5) Belief that God alone is to be worshipped

(6) Belief in prophecy

(7) Belief that Moses was the greatest of the prophets

(8) Belief that the Torah (i.e. Hebrew Scriptures, Old Testament) is eternal

(9) Belief that the Torah is unchanging

(10) Belief that God knows the thoughts and deeds of humanity

(11) Belief that God rewards the righteous and punishes the wicked

(12) Belief in the coming of the Messiah

(13) Belief in the resurrection of the dead

In the main, while there continue to be differences of understanding regarding these various principles across cultural, denominational, and historical lines, they represent what the Jewish people continues to believe and affirm—beliefs which, by the way, are not incompatible with but remain the foundation of Christian faith. How pernicious, then, to attack the Jewish religion as odious and threatening to the very underpinnings of Western civilization when the precise opposite is the case: These thirteen religious "gifts" are based upon the sources from which not only Jesus, but the Gospel writers and Paul drew.

As to the lie of the Jewish people foisting upon an unsuspecting people an immoral, pornographic literature, the reader has only to revisit the refutation of Protocol 5 with its discussion of Jewish ethics, and the refutation of Protocol 10 with its discussion of family, to realize the absolute absurdity of this assertion. This claim is wholly incompatible with everything upon which the faith, culture, and heritage of the Jewish people is based. Indeed, standards of modesty in clothing and conduct are an important part of the religious fabric of Judaism.

The other charges leveled in the fourteenth protocol include topics already addressed and refuted, such as the chosen people (3 and 13), Gentiles (4, 5, 11, and 13), and liberty (1 and 12).

Protocol 15

Utilization of Masonry:
Heartless Suppression of Enemies

Outline

- Plots against the Jewish Government to be prevented by heartless killing and exile.
- Merciless measures are evidence of firm authority.
- The sole enemies to this program are the Russian aristocracy, now on the decline, and the Pope.
- Multiplication of Masonic Lodges during the transitory period which leads to power.
- Individual lodges to be centralized under one unknown to any but Jewish sages.
- Political secrets become known through lodge connections.
- The international police.
- Characteristics of those who join secret societies.
- Curiosity the impelling motive.
- Longing for the emotion of success.
- Gentiles discouraged by small things, even cessation of applause.
- Submergence of individualism is an infringement of natural law.
- Gentiles are "seed of cattle."
- Enemies among the Masons die, when necessary, presumably from sickness, and this uproots the heart of protest.
- Prestige of law to be undermined.
- Forecast of future Jewish laws which will demand obedience.
- Those who fall in assisting maturity of Jewish plans will be like soldiers falling on the field of battle.
- The personnel of judges.
- The elimination of liberalism.
- Satisfying the masses.
- Obedience will be universal.
- The King of Israel will be the Patriarch of the wrold.

See original *Protocol* page 192.

Arguments

- When finally we become rulers, by means of governmental *coup d'état* everywhere simultaneously and subsequent to the definite acknowledgment of the worthlessness of existing forms of government (and before this happens, considerable time must pass, perhaps even a century), we will endeavor to prevent all conspiracies against us.
- The organization of any kind of secret society will also be punished by death, and those societies which now exist and which are known to us as having served or are now serving us will be dissolved and their members exiled to continents far removed from Europe.
- Thus we shall deal with Gentiles among the Masons who know too much, and if for any reason we extend mercy to them, they will remain in constant fear of exile.
- In Gentile society, where we have planted such deep roots of discord and Protestantism, it will be possible to restore order only by merciless measures which will demonstrate our absolute authority.
- Meanwhile, however, until our rule is established, we will organize and multiply lodges of Free Masons.
- All knowledge will be centralized under one administrative body known only to us and unknown to the rest, which will consist of our wise men.
- Usually it is the climbers, careerists, and people, generally speaking, who are not serious, who most readily join secret societies, and we shall find them easy to handle and through them operate the mechanisms of our projected machine.
- The Gentiles join lodges out of curiosity or in the hope that through them they may worm their way into social distinction.
- The Gentiles do not yet comprehend, and will not comprehend, that this hobby is a direct infringement of the chief laws of nature whereby from the very creation of the world every entity has been constituted unlike every other.
- How far-sighted were our wise men of old, when they said that to attain a serious aim one must not hesitate at the means or count the victims sacrificed for the sake of the cause!
- Death is the inevitable end of everyone.

- Under our influence, the execution of the laws of the Gentiles is reduced to a minimum.
- In this divergence between the Gentiles and ourselves in ability to think and reason is to be seen clearly the seal of our election as the Chosen People, as higher human beings, in contrast with the Gentiles, who have merely instinctive and animal minds.
- When the time of our open rule comes, the time to declare its benefits, we will transform all legislation.
- The chief point in them will be obedience to authority, a teaching which will be brought to the highest degree.
- Abuses of authority on the part of those lower in rank than those of last instance will be punished so mercilessly that everyone will lose the desire to experiment with his power.
- Concealment of guilt, connivance between those in the service of the administration, all this kind of crime will disappear after the first examples of harsh punishment.
- The personnel of our judiciary will not serve beyond the age of fifty-five years.
- At present, Gentile judges make exceptions in many crimes, not having a correct view of their own functions.
- We will eliminate liberalism from all the important strategic positions in our administration for which civil service subordinates receive training.
- In answer to a possible remark that the retirement of old officials will be an expense to the treasury, I may state first that private work will be found to reimburse them for that which they are losing; and second, I may remark that all the world's money will be concentrated in our hands, consequently our government need not fear expense.
- Our absolutism will be consistent in every respect, and consequently our authority will be respected and our orders executed in detail.
- We will abolish the right of appeal which will pass exclusively to our jurisdiction—to the immediate cognizance of the ruler, for we must not permit the suspicion to arise among the people that an incorrect decision could be rendered by the judges appointed by us.
- Our government will have the appearance of a patriarchal, paternal guardianship on the part of our ruler.

- As you see, our despotism is based on right and duty; the right to compel the performance of duty is the direct function of government, acting as a father to its subjects.
- Personalities must be sacrificed without hesitation, especially violators of established order, for in punishing evil as an example lies a great educational opportunity.
- When the king of Israel places the crown offered him by Europe on his holy head, he will be proclaimed the patriarch of the world.
- Our ruler will be in constant touch with his people, delivering speeches that will be transmitted immediately to all parts of the world.

Refuting Protocol 15

Israel's alleged blatant contempt for non-Jews, which pervades this protocol, has already been addressed in the refutations to *Protocols* 4, 11, 13, and 14 and need not be repeated here. Suffice it to say that these charges are not only *not* representative of the Jewish experience, but are patently perversions of its history and traditions.

Throughout Jewish history, but most especially during times of intercommunal harmony and tranquility, relations between Jews and non-Jews have been open, mutually receptive, and mutually beneficial. During these same periods, non-Jews wishing to embrace the Jewish religious faith, heritage, and tradition have been warmly welcomed into the House of Israel, and neither they, nor successive generations, suffered any impediments whatsoever. This attitude of accepting the *ger*, convert, as an equal into the Jewish community is as old as the Jewish community and its Torah. In Leviticus (19:33–34) we read, "When a stranger resides in your land, you shall not wrong him. The stranger who resides with you shall be to you as one of your citizens; you shall love him as yourself, for you were strangers in Egypt." The rabbis of the Talmud extended this commandment even further: "Rabbi Meir used to say: a Gentile [who] occupies himself with the study of the Torah . . . equals the high priest" (BT Baba Kamma 38a, ed. Soncino, p. 214), and they even attributed God's special favor to the convert: "The Lord, blessed be He, greatly loves the proselytes" (Numbers Rabbah, Naso 8:2–4, which contains an extended description of the merits of the proselyte; ed. Soncino, p. 204). On the other hand, non-Jews who chose to convert to Judaism have often found themselves experiencing the same kind of discrimination as those born into the Jewish people, even to the extent of being martyred for their new faith.

The notion of one "grand" secretive Masonic lodge guided by the sages of Israel, which was powerful enough to restructure and direct the entire organization of Masonry, has already been definitively countered in the refutations of *Protocols* 9 and 11.

What is even more absurd, however, is the total misunderstanding and demonization of the role of the sages of Israel and the respect with which they are held even now, by the Jewish people. Throughout Jewish history, there have been men of immense learning, spirituality, piety, and religiosity who have continually placed the needs of the Jewish people above their own. From the scribes of the biblical period to the heads of the rabbinical academies in Palestine and Babylonia, including the hundreds of teachers whose names and insights populate the five-hundred-year span of talmudic literature, and down through the ages to the rabbis of the modern period, these men (and now women) continue to be persons of moral integrity and deep wisdom. Their knowledge and integrity earns them the trust of their contemporaries, and their following among the people.

Throughout the long years of Jewish history, rabbis have applied their scholarship and piety to help shape and guide the Jewish experience to meet the changing demands and needs of the internal Jewish community and the larger society. At no time whatsoever has their concern for the physical survival of the Jewish people and its religious-ethical way of life been based on the manipulation or denigration of others, especially non-Jews.

The author, or authors, of this protocol attributes non-existent political power and authority to the Jewish people over the larger non-Jewish population. Such a false perception of the Jewish past and present would be laughable had it not had such tragic consequences. To be sure, at various times in history, in various countries, individual Jews or small groups of Jews, beginning with Joseph in Egypt, have occupied positions of power and authority in government. However, at no time during the nineteen-hundred-year exile of the Jewish people from its homeland have they ever dominated the government of any country wherein they found refuge. In fact, the opposite has been the case. Numerically speaking, Jews continue to be among the smallest of minority populations in virtually every country where they live. And while the twin myths of "Jewish power" and "Jewish conspiracy" continue to preoccupy the antisemitic mind, the facts have never supported these vile accusations.

Lastly, the ludicrous statement "when the king of Israel places the crown offered him by Europe on his holy head, he will be proclaimed the patriarch of the world" is the stuff of fantasy and science fiction! There is no statement anywhere in the entire body of Jewish literature, religious or secular, that remotely even hints at such a preposterous idea! That for which Jews have always prayed can be found in the words of any *Siddur*, the prayer book of the Jewish people: "On that day God will be One and His Name will be one." This prayer reflects the fervent hope that all humanity will come to know and accept God and take upon themselves the religious and ethical obligations which flow from such a commitment. The prayer extends to all people, not just the nations of Europe. Finally, given the rise to prominence of countries in Asia, Africa, and the Middle East, it is certainly absurd to assume that a crowned ruler from Europe will become ruler of the world.

Protocol 16

The Nullification of Education

Outline

- Nullifying the influence of universities.
- Infiltration of faculties by secret agents.
- Political questions to be excluded from curricula.
- Concoctions of political plans and constitutions by ignoramuses like conjuring comedies and dramas.
- Utopians created by super-education along political lines.
- Study of history warped to suit secret ends.
- Free education to be destroyed.
- Visual education.

Arguments

- To destroy all collective forces except our own, we will weaken the universities, which represent the first stage of collectivism, by turning their educational activities in a new direction.
- We will exclude government law from the curriculum as well as all those subjects which touch upon political science.
- The study of classicism and all studies in ancient history in which bad examples of human activity predominate over the good will be replaced by a program dealing with the future.
- Every person will be educated within strict limitations which will include only the subjects related to the purpose and nature of his own work.
- That the ruler may be firmly installed in the minds and hearts of his subjects, it is necessary to instruct the people during his term of office, both in schools and in public forums, in the importance of his acts as well as his beneficent intentions.
- We will destroy all free education.
- We know from the experience of many centuries that people live and are guided by ideas, that people are imbued with these ideas only by the aid of an education which is provided equally for all ages but naturally by different methods.
- A system of enslaving thought is already in operation through

See original *Protocol* page 202.

so-called "visual education" which will turn the Gentiles into thoughtless, obedient animals who must see in order to understand.

Refuting Protocol 16

The cold-hearted manipulation of the educational system for political ends, especially at the university level, as alleged by this protocol, flies in the face not only of the historic Jewish veneration of learning, but of the Jewish experience throughout the ages.

Building upon the discussion in the refutation of Protocol 9, we can add further that one of the three primary purposes of the synagogue as an institution is to become a *bet midrash*, a house of study and learning. Wherever Jews have lived, the synagogue was a place where young and old come to deepen their awareness and knowledge of their Jewish religious faith, heritage, and tradition. The Talmud, itself an encyclopedic Jewish resource, emphasizes the value of education by setting priorities. "Rabbi Joshua ben Levi said that a synagogue may be turned into a bet ha-midrash" (BT Megillah27a, ed. Soncino, p. 161). The first communal kindergartens are already in evidence in Palestine two thousand years ago, and the rabbis lauded the sage credited with their establishment: "The name of that man is to be blessed, to wit, Joshua ben Gamala, [who] came and ordained that teachers of young children should be appointed in each district and each town, and that children should enter school at the age of six or seven" (BT Baba Batra 27a, ed. Soncino, pp. 105–106).

Even in the desperate conditions of Nazi occupation, Jews did not abandon their commitment to education. A report from the Warsaw Ghetto, in 1941, described this commitment. "Twelve teachers taught in the institution under terrible conditions— without regular classrooms, without benches, books or any teaching aids. . . . [h]ungry, their feet swollen from the cold, the teachers would instruct their pupils, who were as hungry and swollen as they were" (cited in Dalia Ofer, "The Education of Jewish Children in Warsaw during the Nazi Occupation," in J.

Roth and E. Maxwell, eds., *Remembering for the Future: The Holocaust in an Age of Genocide*, vol. I, pp. 289–301).

Not only was education pursued in the ghettos of Europe, but even in the concentration camps there were attempts to keep learning alive. The scholar and survivor David Weiss Halivni movingly recorded his experience in the Gross-Rosen concentration camp when he saw a Nazi guard eating a sandwich wrapped in a page from holy text. "I implored him to give me this *bletl*, this page. . . . He gave me the *bletl* . . . and [it] became a rallying point. We looked forward to studying it whenever we had free time. . . . The *bletl* became a visible symbol of a connection between the camp and the activities of Jews throughout history" (Halivni, *The Book and the Sword*, p. 69).

From such committed Jewish orientations have come both the Jewish parochial educational movements and the synagogue-supplemental educational movements common to all Jewish religious denominations. Throughout Jewish history, the role of the family, particularly the parents, toward the achievement of this priority was both primary and supportive.

The true purpose of education, declares the Bible, is for the entire Jewish people to become "a kingdom of priests and a holy nation" (Exodus 19:6). This attitude is in direct opposition to the false claim of the sixteenth protocol, since "Awe of the Lord is the beginning of knowledge," according to Proverbs 1:7. Throughout the biblical period, and ever since, literacy, the ability to read and write, was stressed.

It is fair to say that the Jewish religion rests on a commitment to a high level of Jewish education for all. Postbiblically, with the canonization and closure of the Bible, the text itself and the growing body of commentaries that now accompanied it became the heart of the Jewish school and home curriculum. Over time, the study of the Talmud, five hundred years in the initial writing, superseded the Bible as the core curriculum; however, a knowledge of the Bible remained a primary component not only of the learning process, but of Talmud study as well. For both, memory and repetition played key roles in the learning process.

Higher Jewish learning, specifically rabbinical academies and seminaries, has a long history among the Jewish people. These are the equivalent of the non-Jewish colleges and universities, and in them the "best and the brightest" traveled as far along the educational learning path as their intellectual resources permitted them. The same holds true today, with the ordination of rabbis the apex of Jewish learning. In the modern period, rabbis combine university training and rigorous Jewish learning, and (parochial) Jewish knowledge as well as secular, non-Jewish knowledge in both the humanities and hard sciences is valued.

The rise of Zionism in the nineteenth and twentieth centuries, culminating in the birth of the State of Israel in May of 1948, has profoundly and positively affected Jewish learning. It has sparked a revival of Hebrew, bringing this most ancient and modern of languages back into daily use and study. Plays, novels, short stories as well as the plastic arts (painting and sculpture) and musical arts have likewise experienced a Hebrew-language renaissance. Now, more Jews and non-Jews can read the sacred literature in its original language.

Additionally, in modern times, perhaps the most creative aspect of Jewish education has been the development of summer camps in all the Jewish religious movements—Reform, Conservative, Orthodox, and Reconstructionist. While enjoying the pleasurable activities usually associated with summer camping, such as sports, swimming, hiking, arts and crafts, these programs also have a distinctly Jewish component tailored to inspire the next generation.

From even this cursory survey, then, the false notion of devaluing education in the service of either political ends or economic gain is truly inconsistent with Jewish values and has no basis whatsoever in Jewish historical or contemporary experience. A people that values education and learning for their own sake as well as for the furtherance of its religious commitment is not a people that would abuse or debase these values.

It should also be noted that at the time of the writing of the *Protocols*, a *numerus clausus* (quota system) that limited the number of Jews who were allowed to enroll in universities existed in many countries in the world, such as Poland, Germany, and even the United States. This historical fact demonstrates the absurdity of the charge of Jewish control of the universities, and further undermines the credibility of the *Protocols*.

Protocol 17

The Fate of Lawyers and the Clergy

Outline

- People chilled by technical jurisprudence and the courts demoralized.
- Lawyers to be deprived of contact with clients and to be hired by the state, thus shortening legal procedures.
- Discrediting the priesthood of the Gentiles, whose influence diminishes daily.
- The cash of the Christian religion.
- Other religions to be handled later.
- Pope's court to be annihilated by an invisible hand and its power undermined.
- The education of youth in intermediary religions.
- Fighting churches by criticism and insinuating disorganization.
- Spying to be laudable.
- Agents from all social classes.
- The Kahal.

Arguments

- The practice of law develops men who are cold, cruel, persistent, and unprincipled, and who take an impersonal and purely legal viewpoint in all cases.
- We have taken good care long ago to discredit the Gentile clergy and thereby to destroy their mission, which at present might hamper us considerably.
- Freedom of conscience has been proclaimed everywhere.
- When the moment comes for the final annihilation of the Pope's court, the finger of an invisible hand will guide the masses in that direction.
- The King of the Jews will be the true Pope of the Universe, the Patriarch of an International Church.
- Meanwhile, we will reeducate the youth to new intermediary religions and finally in ours.

See original *Protocol* page 204.

- Our contemporary press will expose government and religious affairs and the incapacity of the Gentiles, always using expressions so derogatory as to approach insult, the faculty of employing which is so well known to our race.
- Our rule will be justification for the conception of the divinity Vishnu, who is the physical expression of our aim.
- We will see everywhere, without the help of the official police, which according to the laws drawn up by us for the Gentiles is an obstruction to proper government supervision.
- Our agents will be taken from the highest and lowest ranks of society, from the gay [i.e., carefree] administrative classes; they will be editors, typographers, booksellers, salesmen, workmen, coachmen, and footmen.
- Even now, our brothers are under obligation to denounce apostates of their own family or any person known to be opposed to the *Kahal* [i.e., Jewish Community].
- An organization of this character will eliminate all abuse of authority, coercion, corruption, and all those things which have been introduced and accepted by the Gentiles upon our advice.

Refuting Protocol 17

Two statements in the seventeenth protocol reveal (1) the obvious non-Jewish authorship of the document and (2) the ignorance of the author or authors regarding the Jewish religious faith, heritage, and tradition. Before evaluating the protocol itself, let us address these two statements.

"The King of the Jews will be the true Pope of the Universe, the Patriarch of an International Church." In this one sentence alone, we can find three falsehoods!

The phrase "king of the Jews," appears *nowhere* in the Jewish Scriptures, nor anywhere in Jewish religious texts. This phrase is, in fact, a New Testament reference to the sign in Latin (*Rex Judeorum*) fastened at Jesus' feet on the cross which identifies the reason for his crucifixion at the hands of the Romans (i.e., the Roman perception of him as a political revolutionary plotting to overthrow the imposed government).

The phrase "Pope of the Universe" reveals an absolute ignorance of Jewish religious life in that there is no equivalent office
to the pope of the Roman Catholic Church. The chief rabbis in
the State of Israel do not have the universal appeal, influence, or
status of the pope, and, of course, the office of the Chief Rabbi
of Israel did not even exist at the time of the publication of the
Protocols, since it was instituted by the British in Palestine in
1920.

The third phrase, "Patriarch of an International Church," uses
a term for a house of worship common to the Christian communities of faith but in no way *ever* identified with the temples or
synagogues of the Jewish faith.

Thus, the use of the decidedly Christian terms "King of the
Jews," "Pope," and "Church" leaves us with but one conclusion
and one conclusion only: that the author, or authors, of this spurious text, who attempted to pass themselves off as Jews, were
in fact non-Jews ignorant of Judaism, and relying on Christian
language and sources for inspiration!

Were this not enough, we come to an even more absurd sentence: "Our rule will be justification for the conception of the
divinity Vishnu, who is the physical expression of our aim."
That the God of Israel is incorporeal, without bodily form, is a
foundational belief of both Christians and Jews. According to
the Ten Commandments, God was never to be the subject of
physical representation in either painting, drawing or sculpture,
as is well known. Indeed, the fifth of Maimonides' Thirteen Principles of the Jewish Faith, which are recited each day in the daily
prayer service, stresses this belief.

To refer to one of the primary deities of the Hindu religious
tradition as somehow having relevance or meaning for Jews de-
fies any logical understanding of or for what Judaism has stood
for thirty-five hundred years. The Jewish religious tradition is
one of uncompromising monotheism. Therefore, to draw upon
one of the major deities of a polytheistic religious tradition such
as Hinduism makes absolutely no sense whatsoever, and, like
the aforementioned, further confirms the non-Jewish authorship
of the *Protocols*.

Turning now to the document itself, the attacks in this protocol are against (1) lawyers, (2) Christian clergy, and (3) Christian-

ity itself, more specifically Roman Catholicism and its papal structure (rather than Protestantism or Eastern Orthodoxy).

Scholars of Judaism characterized not only the Pharisees, but the early rabbis as "Doctors of the Law" (see, for example, the Christian scholar George Foot Moore's classic *Judaism in the First Centuries of the Christian Era*, vol. 2, p. 183). Although many equated the "Old Testament" primarily as a "book of law" and Judaism as preoccupied with the minutiae of legal matters, and therefore devoid of significant spiritual emphases, they still have always recognized, at the very least, an overriding concern in Judaism with humanity's need for the disciplined ethical behaviors which are at the heart of any healthy society.

Judaism has always placed a strong religious and moral emphasis on right and wrong, law and punishment—not to the exclusion of religious and spiritual matters, but, rather, as the translation of those commitments into performance and the concrete realization of its religious and societal ideals. Thus, the Jewish people, during its long journey through history, has always held in the highest esteem those who practice the legal profession, understanding them, at least biblically, as representing God in human society.

While it is historically true that Jews were denied both the right to become lawyers and to teach law at the university level in most European countries until the nineteenth century, this sad fact has in no way diminished the respect in which both the laws of society and the lawyers and justices who administer them are held. Today, at the start of the twenty-first century, the profession of law and the teaching of law continue to attract an increasing number of Jews. Thus, what has survived is a respect for those committed to the study and practice of law, not to the corruption of the legal system, as this protocol would have the reader believe.

Additionally, the seventeenth protocol's attack upon Christian clergy and Christianity itself, primarily Roman Catholicism and its pope, squares neither with historical fact nor with contemporary reality. To be sure, prior to the latter half of the twentieth century, relationships between Judaism and Christianity and the Jewish people and the various Christian communities of Europe were far more negative than positive, and interaction with representative clergy also typically more negative than positive. But while there does exist a small body of polemical works that attempted to defend Judaism from Christian attacks, the vast majority of Jewish religious texts do not contain any contempt and in fact exist primarily to help the Jew realize the full potential of his or her religious commitment and identity. Indeed, one has only to look at the positive responses from Jews to the gestures of reconciliation from Pope John Paul II to realize how false the picture painted by this protocol is.

The reaction of Rabbi Michael Melchior to the pope's prayer at the Western Wall in Jerusalem is just one example. Melchior said: "When he touched the Wall I sensed that the Wall was indeed moving in the Pontiff's direction. . . . It was as if a door, closed for so many centuries, was starting to open to reconciliation and peace among Christians and Jews" (Melchior, "Opening the Doors to a Peaceful Era," p. 7).

The mushrooming interfaith dialogues which began after the Holocaust and continue to expand even at the present time bring rabbis, scholars, and theologians together with priests, ministers, and other clergy who are truly desirous of learning from one another in an environment of mutual respect. Such dialogues, which more often than not include laypersons as well, exist on local, regional, national, and international levels, and show no signs of abating.

Protocol 18

The Organization of Disorder

Outline

- Bringing order out of chaos by oratory.
- Conspirators work for love of the game and for the sake of talking.
- Authority loses prestige when conspiracies are discovered.
- Conspiracies presume weakness.
- One method of disorganization is to promote treasonable groups and directing their discovery.
- Secret guards for Jewish rulers who are to use their authority for the good of the people.
- No open protection to be used.
- The right of petition and the arrest of criminals.

Arguments

- When it becomes necessary to arrange measures for secret defense [admitting that the need for defense is a most potent poison for the prestige of authority], we will organize upon disorder or the expression of discontent with the cooperation of the best orators.
- As most conspirators work for love of the game and for the sake of talking, until they commit some overt act, we will not disturb them, but we will always keep watchful agents in contact with them.
- Our ruler will be watched only by an invisible guard, because we will not admit that treason is possible, which he is unable to neutralize and from which he is obliged to hide.
- Should we permit this thought, as has been done and is being done by the Gentiles, that of itself would be signing a death-warrant, if not for him in person then in the near future for his dynasty.
- According to a policy which has been planned with strict regard to appearances, our ruler will use his power only for the good of the people and in no case to stabilize his own dynasty.

See original *Protocol* page 207.

- To guard the ruler openly is synonymous with admitting weakness in his political position.
- Our ruler, even among the people, will be surrounded as though by a mob of curious persons, men and women, who will occupy places close at hand.
- With the establishment of open official protection, the mystical prestige of authority disappears.
- At first we will arrest criminals on more or less well-founded suspicion.

Refuting Protocol 18

The only seemingly new thing in the eighteenth protocol is the supposed use of manipulative oratorical skills to keep the non-Jews (Gentiles) in line and bend them to the will and desire of the non-existent Jewish ruling elite. (The whole matter of the supposed Jewish contempt for Gentiles has already been addressed in the refutations to protocols 4, 5, 11, 13, 14, and 15. Other themes found here, such as authority, conspiracy, disloyalty, and power have been answered in the refutations to *Protocols* 1, 2, 7, and 15 respectively.)

Given the respect for the written word which has long been a hallmark of the Jewish religious tradition—the veneration with which the parchment scrolls of the Pentateuch are held being the supreme example—we find a strong sense of responsibility to the spoken word in the Bible itself, as well as in the postbiblical or rabbinic period right up to and including the present day. In fact, the law was originally known as the Oral Law, and was studied and handed down verbally.

Judaism absolutely rejects and forbids the manipulation of speech for negative purposes. Slanderous words, defamation of character, and slurs against a fellow human being are all addressed under the rubric of *lashon ha-ra* (literally "evil speech"). The understanding of the rabbis of the talmudic period and beyond is that such words destroy three people: the one "who tells . . . , [the one] who accepts [the evil words] . . . , and [the one] about whom it is told" (BT Arakin 15b, ed. Soncino, p. 89). Mar the son of Ravina, upon finishing his daily prayers, added the sentence "My God, keep my tongue from evil and my lips from speaking guile" (BT Berachot 17a, ed. Soncino, p. 100), which has become a permanent part of Jewish liturgy, traditionally recited three times daily. In modern times, Rabbi Israel Meir Kagan (1838–1933), a saintly Lithuanian rabbi, published a book devoted to the importance of the Jewish prohibitions against slander. It became a true classic of Jewish religious literature, and continues to exercise a profound influence on today's Jews as well.

Thus, for Jews, the manipulative use of language against one's fellow human beings, Jewish or Gentile, is morally wrong, offensive, and directly contradictory to both the spirit and the words of Jewish teachings.

Protocol 19

Mutual Understanding Between Ruler and People

Outline

- Presentations of petitions encouraged because they disclose trend of thought.
- Disorder turned to mutual understanding.
- Taking away the prestige of martyrdom.
- The clever compilation of books on history.
- Increasing the contingent of liberals and radicals from the ranks of the Gentiles.

Arguments

- Though we will not allow individuals to dabble in political affairs, we will encourage the presentation of reports and petitions which suggest plans for bettering the condition of the people.
- Treasonable gossip is nothing more serious than the barking of a lap-dog at an elephant for a well-organized government, not from the aspect of the police but from the social standpoint.
- To remove the prestige of martyrdom attached to political crimes, we will place transgressors of this character in the same class with thieves, murderers, and all kinds of abominable and disgusting criminals.
- We have attempted, and I hope we have succeeded, in preventing the Gentiles from using this method of resistance against sedition.

Refuting Protocol 19

The nineteenth protocol revolves around the question of Gentile resistance and submission to the nefarious designs of the supposed Jewish conspiracy. We need not dwell here on addressing false claims about Jewish attitudes toward non-Jews, which have already been presented and rebutted in the refutations to *Proto-*

See original *Protocol* page 210.

cols 4, 5, 11, 13, 14, and 15. What is new here, however, are the slanders about Jewish attitudes toward (1) gossip, and (2) martyrdom.

Biblical statements such as "You must not carry false rumors" (Exodus 23:1) and "You shall not go about as a tale-bearer" (Leviticus 19:17) establish concretely Israel's negative attitude toward the gossip-monger. These ultimately lead to legal proscriptions in later literature whereby the rabbis say that someone "who publicly shames his neighbor is as though he shed blood" (BT Baba Metzia 58b, ed. Soncino, p. 348).

In postbiblical and rabbinic literature, the Hebrew phrase most associated with martyrdom is *kiddush ha-Shem*, that is, those willing to die for the sanctification of the Holy Name of God. Traditionally martyrdom has been understood as the willingness to die rather than transgress three religious commandments, those of murder, idolatry, and sexual immorality (BT Sanhedrin 74a, ed. Soncino, p. 502).

The waves of persecution in the early medieval period in Central Europe caused the rabbis to address this issue directly. Rabbi Meir of Rothenburg, who himself was imprisoned until his death in 1293, composed the following: "Blessed art Thou, O Lord our God . . . who has bade us to love Thy glorious and awful name . . . and to sanctify Thy Name in public" (cited in Glatzer, *Faith and Knowledge*, pp. 120–121).

In our modern era, given the complexity of the moral and ethical issues associated with the horror of the Holocaust, martyrdom has also been perceived as the case of the individual willing to give up his or her own life so that the community itself could possibly survive.

That both Jews and Christians throughout their long histories give so much evidence of martyrdom is tribute to the power of their religious messages and teachings, and a denial and refutation of the cynical contempt expressed in this protocol for both communities of faith and for all who act on their ideals.

Protocol 20

The Financial Program of Destruction and Construction

Outline

- Actions to be measured in figures.
- No heavy taxes for self-defense when the Jews become rulers.
- The king will theoretically own everything.
- Progressive tax on property, the rich to bear the heavier part of the burden.
- Guarantees of honest gain.
- Social reform comes from the top, and the time is ripe.
- Taxes on the poor are seeds of revolution.
- Lessening the growth of wealth concentration.
- Present personal tax a means of inciting revolt.
- Financial reports.
- Progressive stamp taxes on property transfers.
- The reserve and the cost of public works.
- Office of accounts.
- Economic crises caused by the Jews by withdrawal of money from circulation.
- The concentration of industry.
- Variable per capita supply of paper money.
- Gold exchange a source of destruction to Gentile governments.
- Discrediting Gentile budgets.
- Loans are the handles for gaining control, by "exhaustion of voluntary blood-letting."
- Debt and government bonds.
- Commercial paper to be purchased by the government.
- "The genius of our chosen kind."
- The accounting system.
- Gentile rules are only screens for destructive programs drawn up by Jewish agents.

Arguments

- Today we will speak of the financial program, the discussion of which I have postponed to the close of my report as it is the most difficult, decisive, and concrete of our plans.

See original *Protocol* page 211.

- When we become rulers, our autocratic government, as a first principle of self-protection, will avoid burdening the people with heavy taxes.
- Our government, under which the ownership of everything in the kingdom will be granted to our ruler by a legal fiction which may be translated easily into fact, can resort to the lawful confiscation of all money in order to regulate its circulation in the kingdom.
- This social reform must come from above, for the time is ripe, and it is necessary as a guarantee of peace.
- A tax on the poor man is the seed of revolution, and it is detrimental to the government which loses the big thing in its pursuit of the small.
- A tax that increases in percentage ratio according to the capital will yield much greater revenue than the present individual or property tax which is useful to us now only as a means of inciting discontent and revolt among the Gentiles.
- The power upon which our ruler will depend consists in the balance and guarantee of peace to attain that which it is indispensable for capitalists to part with of some of their income for the sake of the smooth operation of the governmental machinery.
- Such a measure will destroy the hatred of the poor toward the rich, who will be regarded as the financial support of the government and the exponents of peace and prosperity.
- In order that taxpapers of the educated classes shall not distress themselves about new taxes, they will receive detailed reports of disbursements, exclusive of such monies as may be appropriate to the throne and to administrative institutions.
- The ruler will not hold property in his own name, since everything in the government belongs to him anyway, and the two conceptions are contradictory.
- The relatives of the king, his heirs excepted, who will be supported by the state, must enter the ranks of government officials and work for the right to own property.
- The receipt of purchase money or of an inheritance will be subjected to a progressive stamp tax.
- To what extent such taxes will exceed the income obtained by Gentile governments, it is possible to calculate easily.

- The government must maintain a reserve fund, and all sums in excess must be returned to circulation.
- It should not be implied that even small sums are to be kept in the government treasury over and above a definite and broadly calculated budget, for money should circulate; and to hinder free circulation has a fatal effect upon the government mechanism, which it lubricates.
- The substitution of a part of money exchange by discount paper has created just such an impediment.
- We will establish also an office of accounts where the king will find at all times a complete record of government income and expenses, with the exception of those of the current month, not yet written up, and of the previous month, not yet presented.
- The presence of the ruler at receptions for the sake of etiquette will be eliminated, for much valuable time is thus lost and he needs all for work and thought.
- We have created economic crises for the Gentiles by the withdrawal of money from circulation.
- The present production of money does not coincide generally with the need per capita, and consequently it does not satisfy all the needs of the workingman.
- You know that the gold standard destroyed the governments that created and accepted it, for it could not satisfy the demand for currency, especially as we removed as much gold as possible from circulation.
- We must introduce a unit of exchange based on the value of labor units regardless of whether paper or wood is used as the medium.
- To avoid delay in the payment of money in return for service and supplies to the government, the amounts and dates of payment will be decided by order of the ruler.
- Expense and income budgets will be drafted jointly to prevent lack of balance.
- We will present the plans we have made for reform of the Gentile financial institutions and the principles upon which they are operated in such form that none will be disturbed.
- You may well understand that such a policy, although inspired by us, cannot be followed by us.

- Every loan proves government inefficiency and ignorance of governmental rights.
- What is the ultimate effect of a loan, especially on a foreign loan, other than this?
- It is evident that in establishing an individual tax, the government takes the last pennies of the poor in the form of taxes to return loans to rich foreigners from which the state borrowed money in lieu of gathering those same pennies for its own needs without the payment of interest.
- So long as the loans were domestic, the Gentiles only shifted the money from the pockets of the poor to the coffers of the rich, but when we bribed the necessary persons to make loans in foreign countries, those government treasuries began to pay us a tribute tax which acknowledged their servitude.
- The superficiality of the reigning Gentiles concerning government affairs, the corruption of their ministries, and the ignorance of the rulers of financial problems have forced them to make loans for their countries from our treasuries.
- We will not permit money to stagnate, consequently there will be no government bonds except an issue paying only one percent.
- Commercial paper will be bought by the government, which, instead of paying tribute on loans as at present, will grant loans on a business basis.
- The visual limitation of the purely material minds of the Gentiles is apparent.
- This proves the genius of our minds!
- We will show our accounts at the proper time which will be drawn up in the light of experience gained through centuries of experiments made by us in the Gentile governments.
- We will organize the accounting system so that neither the ruler nor the commonest clerk will be able to deflect the smallest sum from its destination or direct it in a different channel from that indicated in the definite plan of action.
- It is impossible to govern without a definite plan.
- We have led the Gentile kings to neglect government work for grandiose receptions, etiquette, and pleasures which are only screens for our invisible rule.

Refuting Protocol 20

The emphasis of the twentieth protocol is on financial matters, especially (1) taxes and taxation, (2) loans, and (3) bonds, all under the authority of the appointed sovereign, and how these instruments are manipulated to control the overall population. There is no need, however, to again relate the false and deceptive way Jewish/Gentile relationships have been presented throughout this document—and refuted in this study.

The true purpose of these economic discussions, as defined by the author or authors of the *Protocols*, is to substantiate the alleged goal of the Elders of Zion to maintain the inequalities of society, and, if possible, to increase its divisions into the so-called haves (read "Jews") and have-nots (read "Gentiles").

Equally contrary to the picture drawn here, the whole Israelite/Jewish understanding of royalty has a dual emphasis on (1) the humanness of the sovereign, and (2) his obedience to the laws of the nation-state. The Jewish conception of the role of the king has already been fully addressed in the refutation of Protocol 15, and does not need to be reexamined here.

As regards the topic of taxes and taxation, the Jewish people in its literature, both biblical and postbiblical, has confronted this topic and realized in its own journey through history two forms of taxation: (1) internal, administered within the various Jewish communities throughout history for the maintenance and perpetuation of parochially Jewish institutions, such as synagogues, schools, and welfare funds (BT Baba Batra 8a, ed. Soncino, pp. 32–36), and (2) external, those administered by the secular powers of the larger society—country, nation-state, dukedom, province, etc.—for the maintenance of its own institutions as well as for the defense of the realm (BT Baba Kamma 113a, ed. Soncino, pp. 663–664).

Although full citizenship came late to Jews, beginning in France at the end of the eighteenth century, Jews have affirmed the legitimacy of both forms of taxation throughout their evolution as a people even where they were not permitted full participation in the political process. Where it is fairly assessed, both internally and externally, Jews offer no objection whatsoever to the understanding that communal participation and responsibility involve economic participation and responsibility.

Sadly, in the past, especially in Germany and in Russia, mention must be made of the so-called "Jew tax," whereby royal sovereigns unfairly leveled disproportionate taxes upon resident Jewish communities as a means of filling their own treasuries. Such "taxation without representation" was and remains yet another example of antisemitism in practice.

In theory, the notion of a "graduated tax on capital" is economically meritorious, but, as presented here, its purported agenda is an act of deception. It is meant to fool the larger population into falsely believing that the "benevolent sovereignty" of the king and his councilors is for their benefit and protection, whereas the real goal is to rob them of any desire to foment political revolution or rebellion.

This protocol also goes to great lengths to suggest that yet another part of the conspiratorial Jewish economic agenda is to significantly increase the royal coffers at Gentile expense. To be sure, individual Jews in many countries throughout the world may have been or are involved in governmental economic policy. But, with the exception of the State of Israel, the Jewish people as a separate and defined group is nowhere involved economically or politically (or in any other way) in pursuing an independent economic agenda. This is yet another charge that is without any substance whatsoever.

What is, however, most interesting about the twentieth protocol is its discussion of personal income taxes, fair and equitable disbursement of monies collected, fair wages for fair labor, loans to foreign governments (i.e., foreign aid), government borrowing, government bonds, and economic corruption. These are all legitimate issues for debate in any society, especially where the need for goods and services continues to increase as populations grow, and where taxes are unfairly administered or corruption sets in. However, this protocol simplistically seeks to attribute all negative economic activity in any society to a conspiratorial Jewish master plan. This ultimate big lie flies in the face of reality and disregards four-thousand-plus years of Jewish communal history and commitment.

It equally disregards a vast Jewish literature on the subject of loans and bonds, the latter being understood as a type of loan, to which we now turn.

Biblically, it was considered meritorious to lend to the poor with the understanding that the loan would be paid back without pressuring or embarassing the receiver of the loan ("If you lend money to My people, to the poor who is in your power, do not act toward him as a creditor; exact no interest from him," Exodus 22:24). Such mutuality was further stressed in the post-biblical or Rabbinic period, and remains true even today. So important, in fact, did the rabbis of later Jewish religious tradition regard this specific act that among the subjects addressed are the following: (1) nature of the repayment obligation, (2) repayment date, (3) acceptance of payment, (4) method and means of payment, and (5) multiple loans. Nowhere in this vast literature was the lending of money understood as a form of economic oppression.

Relevant to this discussion, therefore, is always the concept of usury and moneylending. The Bible prohibited usury—the charging of unfair interest for the loan of money (Exodus 22:25–26, Leviticus 25:35–37, Deuteronomy 23:19–20). The focus of these passages was twofold: (1) that it was the obligation of those who could afford to do so to lend to those in need, and (2) that interest should not be charged those who could ill afford to pay it. Thus, both biblically and subsequently, such questions had a moral and ethical component.

In the Middle Ages, the Roman Catholic Church viewed these proscriptions against the charging of interest as part of its own moral teachings, and, by extension, of Christianity itself. Yet, with the rise of mercantilism and capitalism, and the lessening power of the Church, the need for credit and capital intensified. Coupled with the exclusion of Jews from owning land and engaging in agriculture and most other occupations and professions, including membership in the various trade guilds, this saw some Jews compelled to turn toward commerce and then to moneylending. Antisemitism played a part in that, early on, Jews recognized the advantage of occupations that would bring them liquid assets (money, diamonds, etc.) that could be used when flight from persecution became reality. This historical reality resulted, most unfairly, in the prejudicial stereotyping of Jews as preoccupied with money, having special skills with regard to money, and the like, all of which contributed to the poisoning of attitudes toward all Jews and culminated in the Holocaust.

Protocol 21

Domestic Loans and Government Credit

Outline

- Profiting by corruption of the administrators and the negligence of rulers.
- Details of the floating of domestic loans.
- Conversions of bonds and methods used to accomplish them.
- Banishment of stock exchanges.
- Legal fixation of the price of stocks.
- Government credit institutions which will increase Jewish power.

Arguments

- To that which I reported to you at the last meeting I will add one more detail concerning domestic loans.
- We have profited by the corruption of the administrators and by the slackness of the rulers to loan sums that have been doubled, trebled, and many times multiplied, loaning Gentile governments money that was absolutely not needed by their states.
- In announcing such a loan, the governments will open subscriptions on their own bills of exchange or bonds.
- But after the comedy has been played, the fact of a deficit emerges, and usually it is a heavy one.
- Then arrives the time for conversions, which decrease payment of interest but which do not cover debts.
- Avowed bankruptcy will thus be the best proof of the breach between the people and their governments.
- I direct your definite attention to these points and to the following: at present all domestic loans are consolidated into so-called floating debts, whose dates of repayments are more or less close at hand.
- When we ascend the thrones of the world, such financial expediences, not being in accord with our interest, will be definitely eliminated.

See original *Protocol* page 219.

- We will replace stock exchanges by great government credit institutions, whose functions will be to tax trade and paper according to government regulations.

Refuting Protocol 21

The twenty-first protocol is simply an extension of the twentieth, and thus there is little (if any) need to refute, still again, such false and malignant items, already addressed, as taxes and taxation, loans and bonds, usury and moneylending.

What is more beneficial, however, is to emphasize the relatively minor and insignificant role Jews have historically played in the creation of stock exchanges and stock markets. This fact runs counter to the long-lived antisemitic assertion that attributes to Jews some secret or special ability with regard to the manipulation of money.

Historically stock exchanges/markets were created only in the late Middle Ages with the rise of mercantilism and capitalism. Some Jews did turn to these activities, first in the Netherlands, then in England and the United States, but they never attained large or dominant positions. In other countries, Jews found their participation blocked. In Germany, for example, with the exception of the privileged "court Jews," Jews were barred until the nineteenth century, when, due to the prominence of such families as the Rothschilds, they began to play an increasingly larger part in commerce and finance, and remained so until the rise of the Nazis in the 1930s. Somewhat parallel situations may be found with regard to the Jews of Poland, Hungary, and Austria. Certainly, as noted above, Jews never were the dominant factors or the only ones to profit and gain large fortunes.

Protocol 22

The Beneficence of Jewish Rule

Outline

- Secrets of past and present events.
- Gold, the greatest modern power, is in our hands.
- Our rule decreed by God.
- The evil which we were forced to do for centuries will result in the evolution of order everywhere and the enjoyment of peace and happiness for the people.
- Freedom is not license to disturb others.
- Our power will rule and guide and will bring order and happiness.
- Power does not bow before any right, even that of God.

Arguments

- In all which I have discussed with you hitherto, I have endeavored to indicate carefully the secrets of past and future events and of those momentous occurrences of the near future toward which we are rushing in a stream of great crises, anticipating the hidden principles of future relationships with the Gentiles and of our financial operations.
- We hold in our hands the greatest modern power—gold; in two days we could free it from our treasuries in any desired quantity.
- Is there a need for us to prove that our rule is predestined by God?
- Our authority will be great because it will be sublime.

Refuting Protocol 22

As we draw near the end of the *Protocols* and their refutations, we again see the author or authors reverting to antisemitic stereotypes and repeating two of the blatantly false charges with which the *Protocols* began: (1) that the Jews' fixation on gold (read "money) is at the root of their conspiratorial attempt to

See original *Protocol* page 222.

rule civilization, and (2) that the Jewish understanding of biblical chosenness is wrong.

According to the author(s) of the *Protocols*, Jews rely on the concept of chosenness to validate their supposedly arrogant attitude toward all non-Jews, along with an elitism that comes from walking with God in a way superior to other human beings. That both of these charges are patently false and have already been specifically addressed in the refutations to *Protocols* 1, 3, and 13 does not minimize the tragic impact they have had, and have the potential to have in the future.

To reiterate a central truth about Judaism and the Jewish people that these truths attempt to obliterate: the responsibility of those in possession of wealth is to use it to be of help to others, coming as it does as a blessing from God. In no way are the less fortunate to be exploited financially or in any other manner for the benefit of the wealthy. This attitude is not only to be found in the Bible but throughout Rabbinic literature and law.

Further, as regards the chosenness or the election of the people of Israel, this, too, has its roots in the Bible, as has been previously noted. However, it is worth emphasizing again that both the Bible and subsequent Jewish literature stress that to be selected by God is to be God's witness to the Divine Reality on earth. Equally, it carries the moral and ethical responsibility to conduct oneself, both individually and collectively, as proper and worthy emissaries of the Divine Presence (the *Shekhinah*). In no way are others to be viewed as less than whole in God's sight, as less worthy of God's grace, or as less open to the Divine Spirit.

Thus, the contempt for the larger society depicted in this protocol stands as far more of an indictment of the author or authors of the text than of the people they falsely accuse of these evil intentions.

Protocol 23

The Inculcation of Obedience

Outline

- Obedience to be instilled through teaching modesty and limiting the production of luxuries.
- Customs, demoralized by competition, to be changed and handicrafts encouraged.
- Lack of work for the people is dangerous to governments.
- People blindly obey a strong and independent hand.
- Raising order out of disorder by force.
- Criminals and followers of liberalism to be swept away.
- Bow before those who carry the stamp of predestination for rule!

Arguments

- To teach the people obedience, they must be trained in modesty, and to accomplish this, the industrial production of luxurious things must be limited.
- A people devoted to handicrafts do not know what it is to be out of work, and this fact ties them to existing conditions and consequently to the power of authority.
- Drunkenness also will be forbidden by law and will be punishable as a crime against the dignity of the people, for drunkards become bestial under the influence of alcohol.
- I repeat, subjects blindly obey only that hand which is strong and entirely independent of them, in which they feel a defense and a support against the blows of social and economic misfortune.
- Present governments are dragging out their existence endeavoring to manage the affairs of a society demoralized by us.
- This chosen one of God is appointed on high for the purpose of breaking those insane forces moved by instinct and not by intellect, by bestiality and not by humanitarianism.
- It is then that we will say to the people:
- "Bow before your God and before His people who carry upon

See original *Protocol* page 223.

their faces the stamp of predestination, to whom God Himself gave His star as a guide that no one but He Himself should free you from these forces of evil."

Refuting Protocol 23

How appropriate is the French cliché, "The more things change, the more they stay the same" in regard to the twenty-third protocol. The three themes it cites are (1) obedience to authority, (2) the reduction of the non-Jewish (read "Gentile") work force to slavery, and (3) the arrogant and false presumption of Jewish destiny to rule over others.

These issues have all been addressed throughout the responses to the protocols. To briefly restate according to both biblical and post-biblical Jewish sources, respect for properly constituted civil and religious authority functions best when it is devoted to meeting the needs of its constituents. The Talmud illustrates this by telling how workers broke a barrel of wine that belonged to one of the rabbis. He then seized their garments as compensation. The workers complained to another rabbi, who ruled that the first rabbi had to return the garments, and then, when the workers complained that they "are poor men, have worked all day, and are in need," the rabbi ordered that the barrel owner had to "go and pay them." "Is that the law?" he asked. "Even so," was the reply, "in order to help you keep (to) the path of the righteous" (Prov. 2:20) (Baba Metzia 83a, ed. Soncino, 475). Furthermore, Jewish tradition has always maintained that all workers, regardless of education or profession, are to be treated with basic human respect and dignity, and compensated accordingly. While biblical Israel did not dispense with the system of slavery, which was prevalent throughout the ancient world, it took giant strides forward to guard against the physical (and psychological) abuse of its slaves. And as the *Protocols* return again and again to their warped understanding of the chosen people concept, it is important to repeat that the notion of chosenness or election, according to Israelite and Jewish precepts, means the acceptance of greater responsibility toward others through the setting of both moral/ethical and religious/ spiritual examples.

With regard to this last point, it is tragically ironic, just after the end of the most bloody of centuries, the twentieth, labeled by some as "the century of genocide," that the arrogance of self-perceived predestination to rule over others, here falsely attributed to a so-called unnamed Jewish conspiratorial leadership, would more aptly fit the bloody careers of the century's three greatest tyrants: Josef Stalin of Soviet Russia, Adolf Hitler of Nazi Germany, and Mao Zedong of Communist China. The British historian Lord Acton's oft-quoted proverb, "Power tends to corrupt and absolute power corrupts absolutely," applies not only in the political sphere but in all spheres of human activity where leadership and/or authority is wrongly perceived as an *unrestricted* "gift from God."

One other image depicted in the *Protocols* demands a response. Jewish religious tradition, like all religious traditions, regards drunkenness and alcoholism as tragic debasements of the human person. They are glorified neither in biblical nor in postbiblical/rabbinic literature. While alcoholic spirits, either "soft" (wine) or "hard" (beer, liquor), are not viewed as evil by Jews, the loss of self-control and surrendering to excess continue to be seen as a negation of human beings "created in the Divine Image." ("When he becomes drunk, he dances like an ape, and utters folly before all, and knows not what he does," Midrash Tanhuma, Noah 13, 21b, cited in C.G. Montefiore and H. Loewe, *A Rabbinic Anthology*, p. 528.)

Protocol 24

The Jewish Ruler

Outline

- Dynastic foundation of King David to be strengthened.
- Only a few individuals to be prepared for this rulership.
- Direct descendants not to inherit the throne if they show signs of frivolity, lenience, or tendencies detrimental to authority.
- Transference of authority in case of incapacity.
- The future to be in the hands of this Jewish Ruler and the three wise men who initiate him.
- Must often appear in public.
- He must not be influenced by passions.
- Personal desires to be sacrificed, and he must be irreproachable.

Arguments

- Now I will discuss the manner in which the roots of the house of King David will penetrate to the deepest strata of the earth.
- A few members of the house of King David, including their descendants, will be prepared for the position of ruler.
- The practical application of all these plans will be taught only to those selected and by means of comparisons drawn from the experience of many centuries, with observations of politico-economic movements and in accord with the social sciences; in short, entirely in compliance with the spirit of the laws irrevocably drawn up by nature for the purpose of regulating human relationships.
- Direct descendants often will be prevented from inheriting the throne if during their periods of study they show signs of frivolity, lenience, or other tendencies detrimental to authority which would make them incapable of government and in themselves dangerous to the calling of a ruler.
- Only those undoubtedly able persons of a firm, even character will receive the reins of government from our wise men.
- In case of illness or lack of willpower or any other form of

See original *Protocol* page 225.

inefficiency, the ruler will be obliged to yield legally the reins of government to new and competent hands.

- The plans of action which may be adopted by the ruler, both those of an immediate nature and those applicable to the future, will be unknown even to those called the closest advisors.
- Only the ruler and the three men who initiate him will know the future.
- In the person of the ruler, with will inexorable over himself and over all humanity, all will see their destiny with her mysterious ways.
- It is understood that the mental capacity of the ruler must correspond with the program of rule.
- To make people know and love their ruler, he must address the people in public places, thus establishing the necessary union between the two political forces now separated from each other by natural fear.
- The Jewish ruler must not be influenced by his passions, especially by sensuality.
- The descendants of the seed of David, the all-world ruler, must sacrifice all personal desires for their people, for they are the support of mankind.
- Our ruler must be irreproachable.

Refuting Protocol 24

The last protocol presents the so-called Jewish ruler, a descendant of the House/Seed of David, sitting upon a throne and initiated into the responsibilities of rulership by three so-called wise men.

The reference to the House/Seed of David actually has significance for both Jews and Christians who await the appearance/return of the Messiah. Both religions agree that he will be a descendant of the royal Davidic house. This is yet another well-known religious tradition with which the author, or authors, of this spurious antisemitic document are obviously familiar, but twisted for his own hateful purposes. Ironically, however, the familiarity of the author(s) of the *Protocols* with this one aspect of Jewish tradition did not extend to another, namely, that the emphatic lesson of the biblical accounts of David was to remind not only the Children of Israel, but all humanity, that whoever rules the people is not above the law but governed by the same moral, ethical, and religious standards that govern the rest of the people. Failure to honor these standards could lead to removal from high office.

One would assume that, if humanity were really facing such a threatening crisis from the so-called Jewish king and his three cohorts, the *Protocols* would have named the culprits so that the threat could be met. The fact that all are unnamed is the ultimate proof positive that this entire document and its overtly hate-filled agenda are without any substance or validity whatsoever. There was no plan, there is no plan, Jewish or other, for any global conspiracy orchestrated by Jews to unite the world under Jewish domination and to control world economies for Jewish benefit. This has not stopped the use of the *Protocols* by an array of Nazi, Neo-Nazi, Islamist, and other personalities and publications.

Tragically, this ill-conceived and ill-crafted work has emerged as the key document for Jew hatred in the last century, instead of being consigned to the lurid fantasies of pulp fiction. The imagery and stereotypes of the all-powerful Jewish cabal concocted in the *Protocols* provide the intellectual underpinning for those searching for reasons to hate Jews. It continues to serve as inspiration for paranoid conspiratorial theorists across the world and on the Internet who seek to attribute all the world's ills to one scapegoat: the Jews.

The *Protocols of the Learned Elders of Zion* exist only on paper and in the minds of antisemites. They cannot be found in the hearts, minds, or actions of a community of faith, a people and a nation who continue to contribute positively to the ongoing progress of civilization through their commitment to the God of Israel, the God of all humanity.

The Protocols *and the Future of Antisemitism*

Simplistic Solutions and Conspiracy Theories

It remains an ongoing tragedy of our world that there will always be those whose own insecurities will lead them to denigrate others, be they individuals or groups, not only in times of economic downturn but in times of prosperity as well. For economic, military, political, religious, or other reasons, throughout history the seeming necessity of scapegoating has occupied a central place in the cultural landscape of Western civilization; and the dominant recipient of such escalating hatred over the last two thousand years has been the Jews.

One now adds to this potent mix and potential for violence the seeming psychological need for simplistic solutions in times of stress, falsely based on a perception of the "other" as far more powerful than is actually the case. This perception smacks of both a political and a psychological paranoia, and that, coupled with the ability to respond to such perceived threats to the so-called natural order, results in theories of conspiracy and the implementation of strategies to combat them. Again, historically speaking, for much of the last two thousand years of Western civilization, it is the Jews who have been subjected to abuse in response to perceived threats to take over the societies and governments of the nation-states where they have been resident. Hence, the antisemitic forgery of *The Protocols of Learned Elders of Zion* and the obvious reluctance of governments and nations to condemn their publication, despite evidence to the contrary and

125

their refutation in courts of law in South Africa, Switzerland, and Russia.

Make no mistake, however: Those who, for whatever reason, hate the Jews will continue to do so and will continue to cite *The Protocols of the Learned Elders of Zion* as one of their principal rationales for that hatred. Others, regardless of their attitudes toward the Jews—from the neutral to the indifferent to the positively disposed—will continue to reject the forged document of the *Protocols* for what it is, having no value whatsoever other than as an historical aberration or "glitch" on the road to civilizational progress. Finally, there are those who are seemingly confused, who have heard of *The Protocols of the Learned Elders of Zion* and the antisemitic materials which accompany them, but have not yet formed their own conclusions: it is to them that this book is addressed, with the strong admonition that they think for themselves, examine the evidence as it is presented, and draw their own conclusions.

Future Victims

It is truly ironic that while other groups have found themselves outside the universe of moral obligation—for example, Blacks, Asians, Native Americans, Hispanics, homosexuals, Jehovah's Witnesses, Roman Catholics, and Mormons—only the Jews have been subject to such blatantly false conspiracy theorizing on the part of their enemies, a kind of pernicious "reverse compliment," if you will. Yet, because there is no sense of internal logic to either prejudice or hatred, it remains quite possible that those who hate the Jews as well as these other groups will tomorrow adapt such notions to them. *The Protocols of the Learned Elders of Zion* will remain within the arsenal of those who specifically hate the Jews, but it is equally possible that the false and malicious arguments of the *Protocols* will be adapted to meet other needs and other agendas. Fear of conspiracies will continue to fuel the anxieties of the hate communities, and there appears to be little evidence to indicate their diminution in the foreseeable future.

What, then, is to be done? First and foremost, in this era of speeded-up telecommunications, global Internet communications, and CNN, the lies presented in this text must not only be refuted, but the refutations must be distributed worldwide, not only in English, but in a variety of languages as well, accompanied by other media as appropriate. People must be able to see the lies for themselves and the refutations of the lies.

Second, we must educate young people the world over to be textually analytical and discriminating when it comes to materials which make startling and/or grandiose claims that serve to divide the human community from itself even further than it has been in the past or which challenge the legitimacy of any group or subgroup.

Third, we must teach the horrors of the past and present—the Holocaust and other examples of genocide—not only to young people, but to adults, and not only in school settings, but in other settings as well, in order to break the cycle of violence associated with hatred and prejudice. If memory is truly the beginning of redemption, then the time is now to begin the process.

Fourth, we can take to heart the words of Nobel laureate and Holocaust survivor Elie Wiesel: "the Holocaust began with words," and collectively reject words of hatred wherever and by whom offered, and become involved in the process of creating our world anew, remembering always the talmudic injunction, "He who saves one life is as if he saved the entire world" (BT Baba Kamma 38a).

Bibliography

Texts of the Protocols

Ford, Henry, Sr., publisher. *The International Jew: The World's Foremost Problem.* Abridged. 1 vol., n.d.

Ford, Henry, Sr., publisher. *The International Jew: The World's Foremost Problem.* Reedy, W.V.: Liberty Bell Publications, 1976. Reprint, originally published by the *Dearborn Independent,* Dearborn, Mich. 4 vols.:
1. *The International Jew: The World's Foremost Problem,* November 1920.
2. *Jewish Activities in the United States,* April 1921.
3. *Jewish Influences in American Life,* November 1920.
4. *Aspects of Jewish Power in the United States,* May 1922.

Marsden, Victor E., trans. *The Protocols of the Meetings of the Learned Elders of Zion with Preface and Explanatory Notes.* 1934.

Praemunitus, Praemonitus. *The Protocols of the Wise Men of Zion. Translated from the Russian to English Language for the Information of all TRUE AMERICANS & to Confound Enemies of Democracy & the REPUBLIC also to Demonstrate the Possible Fulfillment of Biblical Prophecy as to World Domination by the Chosen People.* New York: Beckwith Co., 1920.

Books, Articles, and Pamphlets

An Address Issued by The American Jewish Committee and Nine Allied Organizations as Rebuttal to the Implied Indictment in The Protocols of the Wise Men of Zion. New York: Beckwith, 1920.

An Exposure of the Hoax Which Is Being Foisted upon the American

129

Public by Henry Ford in His Weekly Newspaper Entitled "The Dearborn Independent" and in the Pamphlet Which He Is Distributing Entitled "The World's Foremost Problem". Chicago: Anti-Defamation League, n.d.

Bat Ye'or. "Islam: History and Taboo." *Midstream*, February–March 1998, p. 7.

Baldwin, Neil. *Henry Ford & the Jews: The Mass Production of Hate*. New York: Public Affairs, 2001

Barkun, Michael. *Religion and the Racist Right*. Chapel Hill: University of North Carolina Press, 1994.

Baron, Salo. "The Modern and Contemporary Periods: Review of the History" in Baron and George S. Wise, eds. *Violence and Defense in the Jewish Experience*, Philadelphia, Jewish Publication Society, 1977.

Ben-Itto, Hadassah. *The Lie that Would Not Die* (Heb.), Tel Aviv: Dvir, 1998.

Bergmann, Werner, and Rainer Erb. *Anti-Semitism in Germany: The Post Nazi Epoch Since 1945*. New Brunswick, N.J.: Transaction Publishers, 1997.

Bergmeister, Karl. *The Jewish World Conspiracy: The Protocols of the Elders of Zion before the Court in Berne*. Reedy, W.V.: Liberty Bell Publications, 1938.

Berkovits, Eliezer. *Not in Heaven: The Nature and Function of Halakhah*. New York: KTAV, 1983.

Berman, Paul. "The Other and the Almost Same." *New Yorker*, February 28, 1994, vol. 70, pp. 61–71.

Bernstein, Herman. *The History of a Lie: "The Protocols of the Wise Men of Zion."* New York: J. S. Oglivie, 1928.

———. *The Truth About "The Protocols of Zion": A Complete Exposure*. New York: KTAV, 1971.

Blackmer, Rollin C. *The Lodge and the Craft: A Practical Explanation of the Work of the Freemasonry*. Richmond, Va.: Macoy Publishing and Masonic Supply Co., 1976.

Blee, Kathleen. *Inside Organized Racism*. Berkeley: University of California Press, 2002.

Boston, Robert. *The Most Dangerous Man in America? Pat Robertson and the Rise of the Christian Coalition*. Amherst, Mass.: Prometheus Books, 1996.

Brackman, Harold. *Farrakhan's Reign of Historical Error: The Truth*

Behind "The Secret Relationship Between Blacks and Jews." Los Angeles: Simon Wiesenthal Center, 1992.

Bronner, Stephen Eric. *A Rumor About the Jews: Reflections on Antisemitism and the Protocols of the Learned Elders of Zion.* New York: St. Martins, 2000.

Cantor, David. *The Religious Right: The Assault on Tolerance & Pluralism in America.* New York: Anti-Defamation League, 1994.

Caplan, Marc. *Jew-Hatred as History: An Analysis of Islam's "The Secret Relationship Between Blacks and Jews."* New York: Anti-Defamation League, 1993.

Carmichael, Joel. *The Satanizing of the Jews: Origin and Development of Mystical Anti-Semitism.* New York: Fromm International Publishing Corp., 1992.

Cecil, Robert. *The Myth of the Master Race: Alfred Rosenberg and Nazi Ideology.* New York: Dodd, Mead, 1972.

Chandler, Albert R. *Rosenberg's Nazi Myth.* New York: Greenwood Press, 1968.

Charles, Pierre. "The Learned Elders of Zion" in John Oesterreicher, ed., *The Bridge,* vol. 1. New York: Pantheon, 1955, pp. 159–188.

"Charter of Islamic Resistance Movement—Hamas/Gaza, August 1988, Selected Translations and Analysis." Los Angeles: Simon Wiesenthal Center, 1988.

Chazan, Robert. *European Jewry and the First Crusade.* Berkeley: University of California Press, 1996.

Chazan, Robert. *Medieval Stereotypes and Modern Antisemitism.* Berkeley: University of California Press, 1997.

Clarkson, Frederick. *Eternal Hostility: The Struggle Between Theocracy and Democracy.* Monroe, Me: Common Courage Press, 1997.

Cohn, Norman. *Warrant for Genocide: The Myth of the Jewish World Conspiracy and The Protocols of the Elders of Zion.* New York: Harper & Row, 1967.

Coleman, John. *Conspirator's Hierarchy: The Story of the Committee of 300.* Carson City, Nev.: America West Publishers, 1992.

Cooper, Abraham. *Portraits of Infamy: A Study of Antisemitic Caricatures and Their Roots in Nazi Ideology.* Los Angeles: Simon Wiesenthal Center, 1987.

———. *Portraits of Infamy: Catalogue and Source Book.* Los Angeles: Simon Wiesenthal Center, 1986.

Cooper, Milton William. *"Behold a Pale Horse."* Sedona, Ariz.: Light Technology Publishing, 1991.

Corcoran, James. *Bitter Harvest: Gordon Kahl and the Posse Comitatus: Murder in the Heartland.* New York: Penguin Books, 1990.

Coughlin, Charles E. *Money! Questions and Answers.* (n.d.)

Coppola, Vincent. *Dragons of God: A Journey Through Far Right America.* Atlanta: Longstreet Press, 1996.

Cremoni, Lucilla. "Antisemitism and Populism in the United States in the 1930's: The Case of Father Coughlin." *Patterns of Prejudice* 32, no. 1 (January 1998): 25–37.

Creutz, W. "New Light on the *Protocols*: Latest Evidence on the Veracity of This Remarkable Document." Reedy, W.V.: Liberty Bell Publications, n.d. Posted by Harold A. Covington in support of the program and goals of the National Socialist White People's Party (nswpp@ix.netcom.com).

Curtiss, John S. *An Appraisal of the PROTOCOLS OF ZION.* New York: Columbia University Press, 1942.

Czackes-Charles, Sacha. "History's Greatest Hoax." *Jewish Times,* London, December 21, 1934, pp. 3, 29.

Daniel, John. *Scarlet and the Beast.* Tyler, Tx.: JKI Publishing. 3 vols.

1. *A History of the War Between English and French Freemasonry* (1995).
2. *English Freemasonry, Mother of Modern Cults Vis-à-vis Mystery Babylon, Mother of Harlots* (1994).
3. *English Freemasonry, Banks, and the Illegal Drug Trade* (1995).

Daraul, Arkon. *A History of Secret Societies.* Secaucus, N.J.: Carol Publishing Group, 1989.

DeLillo, Don. *Underworld.* New York: Scribner, 1997.

Diamond, Sara. *Facing the Wrath: Confronting the Right in Dangerous Times.* Monroe, Me: Common Courage Press, 1996.

Dinnerstein, Leonard. "When Henry Ford Apologized to the Jews." *Moment Magazine,* February 1990, vol. 15, pp. 21–27, 54–55.

———. *Antisemitism in America.* New York: Oxford U. Press, 1994.

Eaton, Richard and Weitzman, Mark. *The New Lexicon of Hate: The Changing Tactics, Language and Symbols of America's Extremists.* Los Angeles: Simon Wiesenthal Center, 1998.

Eco, Umberto. *Serendipities: Language and Lunacy.* Phoenix, London, 1999.

Elliott, Paul. *Brotherhoods of Fear: A History of Violent Organizations.* London: Blanford, 1998.

Evanzz, Karl. *The Messenger: The Rise and Fall of Elijah Muhammad.* New York: Pantheon, 1999.

Ezekiel, Raphael S. *The Racist Mind: Portraits of American Neo-Nazis and Klansmen.* New York: Viking Press, 1995.

False Patriots: The Threat of Antigovernment Extremists. Montgomery, Ala.: Southern Poverty Law Center, 1997.

Ferrand, Pierre. "The Continued Impact of the *Protocols.*" *Midstream,* February–March 1998, vol. 44, pp. 17–20.

Flynn, Kevin, and Gary Gerhardt. *The Silent Brotherhood: Inside America's Racist Underground.* New York: Free Press, 1989.

Funkenstein, Amos. "Theological Responses to the Holocaust" in Funkenstein, *Perceptions of Jewish History*, Berkeley: University of California Press, 1993.

Garber, Jane. "Anti-Semitism and the Muslim World" in David Berger, ed. *History & Hate: The Dimensions of Anti-Semitism.* Philadelphia: Jewish Publication Society, 1986.

Ginsberg, Benjamin. *The Fatal Embrace: Jews and the State: The Politics of Anti-Semitism in the United States.* Chicago: University of Chicago Press, 1993.

Ginzburg, Carlo. *Ecstasies: Deciphering the Witches' Sabbath.* New York: Pantheon Books, 1991.

Glatzer, N. *The Rest Is Commentary.* Boston: Beacon Press 1961.

———. *The Jew in the Medieval World: Faith and Knowledge.* Boston: Beacon Press, 1963.

———. *The Dynamics of Emancipation: The Jew in the Modern Age.* Boston: Beacon Press, 1965.

Glinert, Lewis. "Hebrew." In Arthur A. Cohen and Paul Mendes Flohr, eds., *Contemporary Jewish Religious Thought.* New York: Free Press, 1987.

Goldin, Judah. *The Living Talmud: The Wisdom of the Fathers.* New York: New American Library, 1964.

Goodman, David G., and Miyazawa Masanori. *Jews in the Japanese Mind: The History and Uses of a Cultural Stereotype.* New York: Free Press, 1995.

Grayzel, Solomon. *The Church and the Jews in the XIII Century.* Vol. 2. New York: Wayne State University Press, 1984.

Griffin, Des. *Descent into Slavery?* Clackamas, Or.: Emissary Publications, 1994.

———. *The Fourth Reich of the Rich*. Clackamas, Emissary Publications: Or., 1980.

Gwyer, John. *Portraits of Mean Men: A Short History of the Protocols of the Elders of Zion*. London: Cobden-Sanderson, 1938.

A Different Night: The Family Participation Haggadah. Zion, Noam, and Dishon, David. Jerusalem: Shalom Hartman Institute, 1997.

Halivni, David Weiss. *The Book and the Sword*. New York: Farrar, Straus and Giroux, 1996.

Hamas Charter, selected translations and analysis, Los Angeles, Simon Wiesenthal Center, 1988.

Hard, William. *The Great Jewish Conspiracy*. New York: American Book Co., 1920.

Harris, Geoffrey. *The Dark Side of Europe: The Extreme Right Today*. New York: Barnes & Noble, 1990.

Hawley, Noah. *A Conspiracy of Tall Men*. New York: Harmony Books, 1998.

Heiden, Konrad. *Der Fuehrer*. Boston: Houghton Mifflin, 1944.

Heschel, Abraham Joshua. *The Insecurity of Freedom*. New York: Schocken Books, 1975.

Hockenos, Paul. *Free to Hate: The Rise of the Right in Post-Communist Eastern Europe*. New York: Routledge, 1993.

Hoffman, David. *The Oklahoma City Bombing and the Politics of Terror*. Venice, Ca.: Feral House, 1998.

Hoffman, David S. *High-Tech Hate: Extremist Use of the Internet*. New York: Anti-Defamation League, 1997.

———. *The Web of Hate: Extremists Exploit the Internet*. New York: Anti-Defamation League, 1996.

Hofstadter, Richard. *Anti-intellectualism in American Life*. New York: Alfred A. Knopf, 1963.

———. *The Paranoid Style in American Politics and Other Essays*. New York: Alfred A. Knopf, 1965.

Horowitz, Ariel. "The Jew as 'Destroyer of Culture' in National Socialist Ideology." *Patterns of Prejudice* 32, no. 1 (1998): 51–67.

Icke, David. . . . *And the Truth Shall Set You Free*. Cambridge: Papworth Press, 1995.

Ignatieff, Michael. *Blood and Belonging: Journeys into the New Nationalism.* New York: Farrar, Straus & Giroux, 1993.

Jacobs, Louis. *The Jewish Religion: A Companion.* Oxford: Oxford University Press, 1995.

Jacobson, Kenneth. *The Protocols: Myth and History.* New York: Anti-Defamation League, 1981.

Jeansonne, Glen. *Women of the Far Right.* Chicago. University of Chicago Press, 1996.

Johnson, George. *Architects of Fear: Conspiracy Theories and Paranoia in American Politics.* Los Angeles: Jeremy P. Tarcher, 1983.

Katz, David S., and Popkin, Richard H. *Messianic Revolution: Radical Religious Politics to the End of the Second Millenium.* New York: Hill & Wang, 1998.

Katz, Jacob. *Jews and Freemasons in Europe, 1723–1939.* Cambridge, Ma.: Harvard University Press, 1970. Translated from the Hebrew by Leonard Oschry.

Kertzer, David I. *The Popes Against the Jews.* New York: Alfred A. Knopf, 2001.

King, Christine Elizabeth. *The Nazi State and the New Religions: Five Case Studies in Non-Conformity.* Lewiston, N.Y.: Edwin Mellen Press,1982.

Kinsella, Warren. *Web of Hate: Inside Canada's Far Right Network.* Toronto: Harper Collins, 1994.

Klein, Henry H. *A Jew Exposes the Jewish World Conspiracy.* Reedy, W.V.: Liberty Bell Publications, 1946.

———. *Zionism Rules the World.* Reedy, W.V.: Liberty Bell Publications, 1955.

Knight, Christopher, and Robert Lomas. *The Hiram Key: Pharaohs, Freemasons and the Discovery of the Secret Scrolls of Jesus.* London: Arrow Books, 1997.

Knight, Stephen. *The Brotherhood: The Secret World of the Freemasons.* New York: Dorset Press, 1984.

Krief, A. H. *The Satori and the New Mandarins.* Tampa: Halberg Publishing Corp., 1997.

Kuttner, Paul. *The Holocaust: Hoax or History? The Book of Answers to Those Who Would Deny the Holocaust.* New York: Dawnwood Press, 1996.

Lamy, Philip. *Millennium Rage: Survivalists, White Supremacists, and the Doomsday Prophecy.* New York: Plenum Press, 1996.

Landes, Daniel. "Spiritual Responses in the Ghetto." In *Genocide,* ed. Landes and Alex Grobman. Los Angeles and Chappaqua, N.Y.: S.W.C. & Rossel Books, 1983.

Lapin, Daniel. *America's Real War*. Sisters, Or.: Multnomah Publishers, 1999.

Laqueur, Walter. *Black Hundred: The Rise of the Extreme Right in Russia*. New York: HarperCollins, 1993.

———. *Russia and Germany: A Century of Conflict*. New Brunswick, N.J.: Transaction Publishers, 1990.

Larsson, Goran. *Fact or Fraud? Protocols of the Elders of Zion*. Jerusalem: AMI-Jerusalem Center for Biblical Studies and Research, 1994.

Lee, Albert. *Henry Ford and the Jews*. New York: Stein & Day, 1980.

Lee, Martin. *The Beast Awakens*. Boston: Little, Brown, 1997.

Levinsohn, Florence Hamlish. *Looking for Farrakhan*. Chicago: Ivan R. Dee, 1997.

Lewis, Bernard. *Semites and Anti-Semites*. Norton, N.Y. and London, 1986.

Linzer, Lori, and Marilyn Mayo. *Explosion of Hate: The Growing Danger of the National Alliance*. New York: Anti-Defamation League, 1998.

Lipstadt, Deborah. *Denying the Holocaust: The Growing Assault on Truth and Memory*. New York: Free Press, 1993.

Livingston, Sigmund. *Protocols of the Wise Men of Zion: A Spurious and Fraudulent Document Manufactured to Deceive and to Engender Religious and Racial Hatred*. n.d. (Chicago: Educational Commision of B'nai B'rith [Internet]).

McLamb, Jack. *Operation Vampire Killer Two Thousand: American Police Action Plan for Stopping World Government Rule*. Phoenix: Police Against the New World Order, 1992.

Machiavelli, Niccolo. *The Prince*. New York: Alfred A. Knopf, 1992. Translated by W. K. Marriott.

Mackey, Albert. *The History of Freemasonry: Its Legendary Origins*. New York: Grammercy Books, 1996.

Magida, Arthur J. *Prophet of Rage: A Life of Louis Farrakhan and His Nation*. New York: Basic Books, 1996.

Marschalko. *The World Conquerors: The Real War Criminals*. London: Joseph Sueli Publications, 1958. Translated from the Hungarian by A. Suranyi.

Martin, Tony. *The Jewish Onslaught: Despatches from the Wellesley Battlefront*. Dover, Md.: Majority Press, 1993.

Melchior, Michael. "Opening the Doors to a Peaceful Era." *SIDIC* 34, no. 1 (2001).

Merkl, Peter H., and Leonard Weinberg, eds. *The Revival of Right-Wing Extremism in the Nineties*. London: Frank Cass, 1997.

Midrash Rabbah. London: Soncino Press, 1983.

Mintz, Frank P. *The Liberty Lobby and the American Right: Race, Conspiracy and Culture*. Westport, Conn.: Greenwood Press, 1985.

Mishnah. Oxford: Oxford University Press, 1933. Translated by Herbert Danby.

Mishnah. Jerusalem and Tel Aviv: Bialik Institute, Dvir, 1952–59. Edited by Hanokh Albeck.

Moore, George F. *Judaism in the First Century of the Christian Era*. Cambridge, Ma.: Harvard University Press, 1946.

Montefiore, Claude G., and Herbert Loewe. *A Rabbinic Anthology*. New York: Meridien, 1963.

Mullins, Eustace. *The World Order: Our Secret Rulers*. Staunton, W.V.: Ezra Pound Institute of Civilization, 1984.

Newman, Elias. *The Jewish Peril and the Hidden Hand: The Exposure of a Fraud with a Message to the Jews*. Minneapolis: Hebrew Christian Group, 1933.

Newport, John P. *The New Age Movement and the Biblical Worldview: Conflict and Dialogue*. Grand Rapids, Mi.: William B. Eerdmans, 1998.

Nicolov, Nicola M. *The World Conspiracy: What Historians Won't Tell You!* Portland, Or.: TOPS, 1991.

Nova, Fritz. *Alfred Rosenberg: Philosopher of the Third Reich*. New York: Hippocrene Books, 1986.

Novick, Michael. *White Lies, White Power: The Fight Against White Supremacy and Reactionary Violence*. Monroe, Me.: Common Courage Press, 1995.

Ofer, Dalia. "The Education of Jewish Children in the Warsaw Ghetto During the Nazi Occupation." In *Remembering for the Future: The Holocaust in an Age of Genocide*, ed. J. Roth and E. Maxwell. Palgrave, 2001.

O'Leary, Stephen D. *Arguing the Apocalypse: A Theory of Millenial Rhetoric*. New York: Oxford University Press, 1994.

Ostow, Mortimer. *Myth and Madness: The Psychodynamics of Anti-semitism.* New Brunswick, NJ. Transaction Publishers, 1996.

The Oxford Dictionary of the Jewish Religion. Werblowsky, R. J. and Geoffrey Wigoder, eds. Oxford, New York: Oxford University Press, 1997.

Pipes, Daniel. *Conspiracy: How the Paranoid Style Flourishes and Where It Comes From.* New York: Free Press, 1997.

———. *The Hidden Hand: Middle East Fears of Conspiracy.* New York: St. Martin's Press, 1996.

The "Protocols", Bolshevism, and the Jews: An Address to Their Fellow-Citizens by American Jewish Organizations. 1920.

Rappoport, Jon. "Lifting the Veil: David Icke Interview." *Truth Seeker,* 1998.

Ravitsky, Aviezer. *Freedom Inscribed: Diverse Voices of Jewish Religious Thought.* Tel Aviv: Am Oved, 1999.

———. "Peace" in Arthur A. Cohen and Paul Mendes Flohr, eds. *Contemporary Jewish Religious Thought.* New York: Free Press, 1987.

Ribuffo, Leo. *The Old Christian Right: The Protestant Far Right from the Great Depression to the Cold War.* Philadelphia: Temple University Press, 1983.

Ridgeway, James. *Blood in the Face: The Ku Klux Klan, Aryan Nations, Nazi Skinheads, and Rise of a New White Culture.* New York: Thunder Mouth Press, 1995.

Robert, J. M. *The Mythology of Secret Societies.* New York: Charles Scribner's Sons, 1972.

Robertson, Pat. *The New World Order.* Dallas: Word Publishing, 1991.

Robins, Robert S., and Jerold M. Post. *Political Paranoia: The Psychopolitics of Hatred.* New Haven: Yale University Press, 1997.

Robinson, John J. *Born in Blood: The Lost Secrets of Freemasonry.* New York: M. Evans, 1989.

Rockaway, Robert A. *"The Jews Cannot Defeat Me": The Anti-Jewish Campaign of Louis Farrakhan and the Nation of Islam.* Tel Aviv: Tel Aviv University Press, 1995.

Rosenbaum, Ron. *Explaining Hitler.* New York: Harper Perennial, 1999.

Rosenthal, Bernice Glatzer, ed. *The Occult in Russian and Soviet Culture.* Ithaca, N.Y.: Cornell University Press, 1997.

Sargent, Lyman Tower, ed. *Extremism in America: A Reader*. New York: New York University Press, 1995.

Schmidt, Hans. *End Times/End Games: The Last Months of the Jewish Century*. Pensacola, Fla.: Self-published, 1999.

Schom, Alan Morris. *Survey of Nazi and Pro-Nazi Groups in Switzerland, 1930–1945*. Los Angeles: Simon Wiesenthal Center, 1998.

Segal, Benjamin W. *A Lie and A Libel: The History of the Protocols of the Elders of Zion*. Lincoln: University of Nebraska Press, 1995. Translated and edited by Richard S. Levy.

Shamir, Shimon. "Muslim-Arab Attitudes Toward Jews: The Ottoman and Modern Periods" in Salo W. Baron and Geore S. Wise, eds., *Violence and Defense in the Jewish Experience*. Philadelphia: Jewish Publication Society, 1977.

Shermer, Michael. *Why People Believe Things*. New York: W. H. Freeman, 1997.

Shnirelman, Victor A. *Russian Neo-Pagan Myths and Antisemitism*. Jerusalem: Hebrew University, Vidal Sassoon International Center for the Study of Antisemitism, 1998.

Short, Martin. *Inside the Brotherhood: Future Secrets of the Freemasons*. New York: Dorset Press, 1989.

Simon, Jeffrey D. *The Terrorist Trap: America's Experience with Terrorism*. Bloomington: Indiana University Press, 1994.

Siphre D'Be Rab. H. S. Horovitz, ed. Jerusalem: Wahrmann Books, 1966.

Smith, Brent L. *Terrorism in America: Pipe Bombs and Pipe Dreams*. Albany: State University of New York Press, 1994.

Stern, Kenneth S. *Holocaust Denial*. New York: American Jewish Committee, 1993.

Stern, Kenneth S. *A Force Upon the Plain: The American Militia Movement and the Politics of Hate*. New York: Simon & Schuster, 1996.

Tabor, James D., and Eugene V. Gallagher, *Why Waco? Cults and the Battle for Religious Freedom in America*. Berkeley: University of California Press, 1995.

The Secret Relationship Between Blacks and Jews. Vol. 1. Boston: The Nation of Islam, 1991.

Tosefta. Ed. Saul Lieberman. New York: Jewish Theological Seminary of America, 1973.

Trachtenberg, Joshua. *The Devil and the Jews*. New Haven: Yale University Press, 1943.

Twersky, I. *Introduction to the Code of Maimonides* (Mishneh Torah) New Haven: Yale University Press. 1980.

Valentin, Hugo. *The Protocols of the Elders of Zion*. New York: Viking Press, n.d. (offprint from his book *Antisemitism*).

Wadlow, Rene, and David Littman. "UN Special Rapporteur Censured on Islamist and Arab Antisemitism." *Midstream*, February–March 1998, vol. 44, pp. 8–12.

Webb, James. *The Occult Establishment*. La Salle, Ill.: Open Court, 1976.

Weeks, Theodore R., "The International Jewish Conspiracy Reaches Poland: Teodor Jeske-Choinski and His Works," *East European Quarterly* 30, no. 1 (March 1997): 21–41.

Wegner, Gregory Paul. *Anti-Semitism and Schooling in the Third Reich*. New York and London: Routledge Falmer, 2002.

Weimann, Gabriel, and Conrad Winn. *Hate on Trial: The Zundel Affair, The Media, and Public Opinion in Canada*. Oakville, Ont.: Mosaic Press, 1986.

Weitzman, Mark. "The Inverted Image: Antisemitism and Anti-Catholicism on the Internet." In *Proceedings of the Fifth Biennial Conference on Christianity and the Holocaust: Christianity and Judaism: History, the Holocaust and Reconciliation in the Third Millennium*. Lawrenceville, N.J.: Rider University, 1998.

———. "The Internet Is Our Sword: Aspects of Online Antisemitism." In *Remembering for the Future: The Holocaust in an Age of Genocide*, ed. J. Roth and E. Maxwell. Palgrave, 2001.

Western Civilization in Perspective. London: Ad Hoc Publications, n.d.

Whalen, William. *Christianity and American Freemasonry.* San Francisco: Ignatius Press, 1987.

Whillock, Rita Kirk, and David Slayden, eds. *Hate Speech*. Thousand Oaks, Calif.: Sage Publications, 1995.

Williams, Robert H. *The Ultimate World Order: As Pictured in "The Jewish Utopia."* Reedy, W.V.: Liberty Bell Publications, 1977.

Wilmshurst, W. L. *The Meaning of Masonry*. New York: Grammercy Books, 1980.

Wilson, Colin. *The Occult: A History*. New York: Barnes & Noble, 1971.

Wilson, Robert Anton. *Everything Is Under Control: Conspiracies, Cults, and Cover-Ups*. New York: HarperCollins, 1998.

———. *The Illuminati Papers*. Berkeley, Calif.: Ronin Publishing, 1997.

———. *Right Where You Are Sitting Now: Further Tales of the Illuminati*. Berkeley, Calif.: Ronin Books, 1992.

Winrod, Gerald B. *The Truth About the Protocols*. Reedy, W.V.: Liberty Bell Publications, n.d.

Wise, Stephen S. *Henry Ford's Reaction: Some Further Lessons*. New York: Free Synagogue House, 1928.

Wistrich, Robert. *Antisemitism: The Longest Hatred*. New York: Pantheon, 1991.

Wolf, Lucien. *The Myth of the Jewish Menace in World Affairs; or, The Truth About The Forged Protocols of the Elders of Zion*. New York: Macmillan, 1921.

Wolfe, Robert. *Remember to Dream: A History of Jewish Radicalism*. New York: Jewish Radical Education Project, 1994.

Zamoisky, Lolly. *Behind the Façade of the Masonic Temple*. Moscow: Progress Publishers, 1989. Translated from the Russian by Vyacheslav Nemodruk.

Zeskind, Leonard. *The "Christian Identity" Movement: Analyzing Its Theological Rationalization for Racist and Anti-Semitic Violence*. Atlanta: Center for Democratic Renewal, 1987.

Videotapes

Khalid Abdul Mohammed at Howard University, Washington, DC, 16 April 1994. Taped from C-SPAN Television.

Nazis: The Occult Conspiracy. Discovery Channel Video. 60 minutes.

John J. Robinson. *The Freemasons* (The Secret World Series, vol. 1). Toth and Parson Productions, 1995. 56 minutes.

With God on Our Side: The Rise of the Religious Right in America. PBS Video, 1996.

1. *The Early Crusades, 1950–1969*. 55 minutes.

2. *The Zeal of Thy House, 1969–1974*. 60 minutes.

3. *We Are Family, 1974–1980*. 60 minutes.
4. *Prophets and Advisors, 1979–1984*. 60 minutes.
5. *And Who Shall Lead Them? 1985–1988*. 60 minutes.
6. *God's Armies, 1989–1994*. 60 minutes.

The image reflects a classic antisemitic stereotype. England, 1978.

Appendix

---◦◦◦---

PROTOCOLS
OF THE MEETINGS OF THE
LEARNED ELDERS OF ZION

PROTOCOL NO. 1

Right lies in Might. Freedom — an idea only. Liberalism.
Gold. Faith. Self-Government. Despotism of Capital.
The internal foe. The Mob. Anarchy. Politics *versus*
Morals. The Right of the Strong. The Invincibility of
Jew-Masonic authority. End justifies Means. The
Mob a Blind Man. Political A.B.C. Party Discord.
Most satisfactory form of rule-Despotism. Alcohol.
Classicism. Corruption. Principles and rules of the
Jew-Masonic Government. Terror. "Liberty, Equali-
ty, Fraternity." Principle of Dynastic Rule. Annihi-
lation of the privileges of the Goy-Aristocracy (*i.e.,*
non-Jew). The New Aristocracy. The psychological
calculation. Abstractness of "Liberty." Power of Removal of representatives of the people.

. . . . . .Putting aside fine phrases we shall speak of the
significance of each thought: by comparisons and deductions we shall throw light upon surrounding facts.
What I am about to set forth, then, is our system
from the two point of view, that of ourselves and that of
the *goyim* (*i.e.,* non-Jews).
It must be noted that men with bad instincts are more
in number than the good, and therefore the best results

143

in governing them are attained by violence and terroriza-
tion, and not by academic discussions. Every man aims
at power, everyone would like to become a dictator if
only he could, and rare indeed are the men who would not
be willing to sacrifice the welfare of all for the sake of
securing their own welfare.

What has restrained the beasts of prey who are called
men? What has served for their guidance hitherto?

In the beginnings of the structure of society they were
subjected to brutal and blind force; afterwards — to
Law, which is the same force, only disguised. I draw the
conclusion that by the law of nature right lies in force.

Political freedom is an idea but not a fact. This idea
one must know how to apply whenever it appears necessary with this bait of an idea to attract the masses of
the people to one's party for the purpose of crushing
another who is in authority. This task is rendered easier
if the opponent has himself been infected with the idea
of freedom, *so-called liberalism,* and, for the sake of an
idea, is willing to yield some of his power. It is precisely
here that the triumph of our theory appears: the slackened
reins of government are immediately, by the law of
life, caught up and gathered together by a new hand, because the blind might of the nation cannot for one single
day exist without guidance, and the new authority merely
fits into the place of the old already weakened by
liberalism.

In our day the power which has replaced that of the
rulers who were liberal is the power of Gold. Time was
when Faith ruled. The idea of freedom is impossible of
realization because no one knows how to use it with moderation. It is enough to hand over a people to self-
government for a certain length of time for that people to
be turned into a disorganized mob. From that moment on
we get internecine strife which soon develops into battles
between classes, in the midst of which States burn down
and their importance is reduced to that of a heap of ashes.

Whether a State exhausts itself in its own convulsions, whether its internal discord brings it under the power of external foes — in any case it can be accounted irretrievably lost: *it is in our power*. The despotism of Capital, which is entirely in our hands, reaches out to it a straw that the State, willy-nilly, must take hold of: if not — it goes to the bottom.

Should anyone of a liberal mind say that such reflections as the above are immoral I would put the following questions: — If every State has two foes and if in regard to the external foe it is allowed and not considered immoral to use every manner and art of conflict, as for example to keep the enemy in ignorance of plans of attack and defence, to attack him by night or in superior numbers, then in what way can the same means in regard to a worse foe, the destroyer of the structure of society and the commonweal, be called immoral and not permissible?

Is it possible for any sound logical mind to hope with any success to guide crowds by the aid of reasonable counsels and arguments, when any objection or contradiction, senseless though it may be, can be made and when such objection may find more favour with the people, whose powers of reasoning are superficial? Men in masses and the men of the masses, being guided solely by petty passions, paltry beliefs, customs, traditions and sentimental theorism, fall a prey to party dissension, which hinders any kind of agreement even on the basis of a perfectly reasonable argument. Every resolution of a crowd depends upon a chance or packed majority, which, in its ignorance of political secrets, put forth some ridiculous resolution that lays in the administration a seed of anarchy.

The political has nothing in common with the moral. The ruler who is governed by the moral is not a skilled politician, and is therefore unstable on his throne. He who wishes to rule must have recource both to cunning

ing ourselves in the shade; thanks to the Press we have got and to make-believe. Great national qualities, like frankness and honesty, are vices in politics, for they bring down rulers from their thrones more effectively and more certainly than the most powerful enemy. Such qualities must be the attributes of the kingdoms of the *goyim*, but we must in no wise be guided by them.

Our right lies in force. The word "right" is an abstract thought and proved by nothing. The word means no more than: — Give me what I want in order that thereby I may have a proof that I am stronger than you.

Where does right begin? Where does it end?

In any State in which there is a bad organization of authority, an impersonality of laws and of the rulers who have lost their personality amid the flood of rights ever multiplying out of liberalism, I find a new right — to attack by the right of the strong, and to scatter to the winds all existing forces of order and regulation, to reconstruct all institutions and to become the sovereign lord of those who have left to us the rights of their power by laying them down voluntarily in their liberalism.

Our power in the present tottering condition of all forms of power will be more invisible than any other, because it will remain invisible until the moment when it has gained such strength that no cunning can any longer undermine it.

Out of the temporary evil we are now compelled to commit will emerge the good of an unshakeable rule, which will restore the regular course of the machinery of the national life, brought to naught by liberalism. The result justifies the means. Let us, however, in our plans, direct our attention not so much to what is good and moral as to what is necessary and useful.

Before us is a plan in which is laid down strategically the line from which we cannot deviate without running the risk of seeing the labour of many centuries brought to naught.

In order to elaborate satisfactory forms of action it is necessary to have regard to the rascality, the slackness, the instability of the mob, its lack of capacity to understand and respect the conditions of its own life, or its own welfare. It must be understood that the might of a mob is blind, senseless and unreasoning force ever at the mercy of a suggestion from any side. The blind cannot lead the blind without bringing them into the abyss: consequently, members of the mob, upstarts from the people even though they should be as a genius for wisdom, yet having no understanding of the political, cannot come forward as leaders of the mob without bringing the whole nation to ruin.

Only one trained from childhood for independent rule can have understanding of the words that can be made up of the political alphabet.

A people left to itself i.e., to upstarts from its midst, brings itself to ruin by party dissensions excited by the pursuit of power and honours and the disorders arising therefrom. Is it possible for the masses of the people calmly and without petty jealousies to form judgments, to deal with the affairs of the country, which cannot be mixed up with personal interests? Can they defend themselves from an external foe? It is unthinkable, for a plan broken up into as many parts as there are heads in the mob, loses all homogeneity, and thereby becomes unintelligible and impossible of execution.

It is only with a despotic ruler that plans can be elaborated extensively and clearly in such a way as to distribute the whole properly among the several parts of the machinery of the State: from this the conclusion is inevitable that a satisfactory form of government for any country is one that concentrates in the hands of one responsible person. Without an absolute despotism there can be no existence for civilization which is carried on not by the masses but by their guide, whosoever that person may be. The mob is a savage and displays its savagery at every opportunity. The moment the mob seizes freedom in its hands it quickly turns to anarchy, which in itself is the highest degree of savagery.

Behold the alcoholized animals, bemused with drink, the right to an immoderate use of which comes along with freedom. It is not for us and ours to walk that road. The peoples of the *goyim* are bemused with alcoholic liquors; their youth has grown stupid on classicism and from early immorality, into which it has been inducted by our special agents — by tutors, lackeys, governesses in the houses of the wealthy, by clerks and others, by our women in the places of dissipation frequented by the *goyim*. In the number of these last I count also the so-called "society ladies," voluntary followers of the others in corruption and luxury.

Our countersign is — Force and Make-believe. Only force conquers in political affairs, especially if it be concealed in the talents essential to statesmen. Violence must be the principle, and cunning and make-believe the rule for governments which do not want to lay down their crowns at the feet of agents of some new power. This evil is the one and only means to attain the end, the good. Therefore we must not stop at bribery, deceit and treachery when they should serve towards the attainment of our end. In politics one must know how to seize the property of others without hesitation if by it we secure submission and sovereignty.

Our State, marching along the path of peaceful conquest, has the right to replace the horrors of war by less noticable and more satisfactory sentences of death, necessary to maintain the terror which tends to produce blind submission. Just but merciless severity is the greatest factor of strength in the State: not only for the sake of gain but also in the name of duty, for the sake of victory, we must keep to the programme of violence and make-believe. The doctrine of squaring accounts is precisely as strong as the means of which it makes use. Therefore it is not so much by the means themselves as by the doctrine of severity that we shall triumph and bring all governments into subjection to our super-government. It is enough for them to know that we are merciless for all disobedience to cease.

Far back in ancient times we were the first to cry among the masses of the people the words "Liberty, Equality, Fraternity," words many times repeated since those days by stupid poll-parrots who from all sides round flew down upon these baits and with them carried away the well-being of the world, true freedom of the individual, formerly so well guarded against the pressure of the mob. The would-be wise men of the *goyim*, the intellectuals, could not make anything out of the uttered words in their abstractness; did not note the contradiction of their meaning and inter-relation: did not see that in nature there is no equality, cannot be freedom; that Nature herself has established inequality of minds, of characters, and capacities, just as immutably as she has established subordination to her laws: never stopped to think that the mob is a blind thing, that upstarts elected from among it to bear rule are, in regard to the political, the same blind men as the mob itself, that the adept, though he be a fool, can yet rule, whereas the non-adept, even if he were a genius, understands nothing in the political — to all these things the *goyim* paid no regard; yet all the time it was based upon these things that dynastic rule rested: the father passed on to the son a knowledge of the course of political affairs in such wise that none should know it but members of the dynasty and none could betray it to the governed. As time went on the meaning of the dynastic transference of the true position of affairs in the political was lost, and this aided the success of our cause.

In all corners of the earth the words "Liberty, Equality, Fraternity" brought to our ranks, thanks to our blind

agents, whole legions who bore our banners with enthusiasm. And all the time these words were canker-worms
at work boring into the well-being of the *goyim*, putting
an end everywhere to peace, quiet, solidarity and destroy-
ing all the foundations of the *goya* States. As you will
see later, this helped us to our triumph; it gave us the
possibility, among other things, of getting into our hands
the master card — the destruction of the privileges, or in
other words of the very existence of the aristocracy of the
goyim, that class which was the only defense peoples and
countries had against us. On the ruins of the natural and
genealogical aristocracy of the *goyim* we have set up the
aristocracy of our educated class headed by the aristocracy
of money. The qualifications for this aristocracy we have
established in wealth, which is dependent upon us, and in
knowledge, for which our learned elders provide the motive force.

Our triumph has been rendered easier by the fact that
in our relations with the men whom we wanted we have
always worked upon the most sensitive chords of the
human mind, upon the cash account, upon the cupidity,
upon the insatiability for material needs of man; and each
one of these human weaknesses, taken alone, is sufficient
to paralyse initiative, for it hands over the will of men to
the disposition of him who has bought their activities.

The abstraction of freedom has enabled us to persuade
the mob in all countries that their government is nothing
but the steward of the people who are the owners of the
country, and that the steward may be replaced like a
worn-out glove.

It is this possibility of replacing the representatives of
the people which has placed them at our disposal, and, as
it were, given us the power of appointment.

PROTOCOL NO. 2

Economic Wars — the foundation of the Jewish predominance. Figure-head government and "secret advisers."
Successes of destructive doctrines. Adaptability in politics. Part played by the Press. Cost of gold and value
of Jewish sacrifice.

It is indispensable for our purpose that wars, so far as
possible, should not result in territorial gains: war will
thus be brought on to the economic ground, where the
nations will not fail to perceive in the assistance we give
the strength of our predominance, and this state of things
will put both sides at the mercy of our international *agentur;* which possesses millions of eyes ever on the watch
and unhampered my any limitations whatsoever. Our international rights will then wipe out national rights, in
the proper sense of right, and will rule the nations precisely as the civil law of States rules the relations of their
subjects among themselves.

The administrators, whom we shall choose from
among the public, with strict regard to their capacities for
servile obedience, will not be persons trained in the arts
of government, and will therefore easily become pawns in
our game in the hands of men of learning and genius who
will be their advisers, specialists bred and reared from
early childhood to rule the affairs of the whole world. As
is well known to you, these specialists of ours have been
drawing to fit them for rule the information they need
from our political plans from the lessons of history, from
observations made of the events of every moment as it
passes. The *goyim* are not guided by practical use of unprejudiced historical observation, but by theoretical routine without any critical regard for consequent results. We
need not, therefore, take any account of them — let them
amuse themselves until the hour strikes, or live on hopes
of new forms of enterprising pastime, or on the memories
of all they have enjoyed. For them let that play the prin-

cipal part which we have persuaded them to accept as the dictates of science (theory). It is with this object in view that we are constantly, by means of our press, arousing a blind confidence in these theories. The intellectuals of the *goyim* will puff themselves up with their knowledge and without any logical verification of them will put into effect all the information available from science, which our *agentur* specialists have cunningly pieced together for the purpose of educating their minds in the direction we want.

Do not suppose for a moment that these statements are empty words: think carefully of the successes we arranged for Darwinism, Marxim, Nietzsche-ism. To us Jews, at any rate, it should be plain to see what a distintegrating importance these directives have had upon the minds of the *goyim*.

It is indispensable for us to take account of the thoughts, characters, tendencies of the nations in order to avoid making slips in the political and in the direction of administrative affairs. The triumph of our system, of which the component parts of the machinery may be variously disposed according to the temperament of the peoples met on our way, will fail of success if the practical application of it be not based upon a summing up of the lessons of the past in the light of the present.

In the hands of the States of to-day there is a great force that creates the movement of thought in the people, and that is the Press. The part played by the Press is to keep pointing out requirements supposed to be indispensable, to give voice to the complaints of the people, to express and create discontent. It is in the Press that the triumph of freedom of speech finds its incarnation. But the *goyim* States have not known how to make use of this force; and it has fallen into our hands. Through the Press we have gained the power to influence while remainexist. It proves that Dr. Weizmann knows all about the *gold* in our hands, notwithstanding that we have had to gather it out of oceans of blood and tears. But it has paid us, though we have sacrificed many of our people. Each victim on our side is worth in the sight of God a thousand *goyim*.

PROTOCOL NO. 3

The Symbolic Snake and its significance. The instability of the constitutional scales. Terror in the palaces. Power and ambition. Parliaments "talkeries," pamphlets. Abuse of power. Economic slavery. "People's Rights." Monopolist system and the aristocracy. The Army of Mason-Jewry. Decrescence of the *Goyim*. Hunger and rights of capital. The mob and the coronation of "The Sovereign Lord of all the World." The fundamental precept in the programme of the future Masonic national schools. The secret of the science of the structure of society. Universal economic crisis. Security of "ours" (*i.e.*, our people, Jews). The despotism of Masonry — the kingdom of reason. Loss of the guide. Masonry and the great French Revolution. The King-Despot of the blood of Zion. Causes of the invinsibility of Masonry. Part played by secret masonic agents. Freedom.

To-day I may tell you that our goal is now only a few steps off. There remains a small space to cross and the whole long path we have trodden is ready now to close its cycle of the Symbolic Snake, by which we symbolize our people. When this ring closes, all the States of Europe will be locked in its coil as in a powerful vice.

The constitution scales of these days will shortly break down, for we have established them with a certain lack of accurate balance in order that they may oscillate incessantly until they wear through the pivot on which they turn. The *goyim* are under the impression that they have welded them sufficiently strong and they have all along kept on expecting that the scales would come into equilibrium. But the pivots — the kings on their thrones — are hemmed in by their representatives, who play the fool, distraught with their own uncontrolled and irresponsible power. This power they owe to the terror which has been breathed into the palaces. As they have no means of getting at their people, into their very midst, the kings on their thrones are no longer able to come to terms with them and so strengthen themselves against seekers after power. We have made a gulf between the far-seeing Sovereign Power and the blind force of the people so that both have lost all meaning, for like the blind man and his stick, both are powerless apart.

In order to incite seekers after power to a misuse of power we have set all forces in opposition one to another, breaking up their liberal tendencies towards independence. To this end we have stirred up every form of enterprise, we have armed all parties, we have set up authority as a target for every ambition. Of States we have made gladiatorial arenas where a host of confused issues contend.... A little more, and disorders and bankruptcy will be universal.......

Babblers inexhaustible have turned into oratorical contests the sittings of Parliament and Administrative Boards. Bold journalists and unscrupulous pamphleteers daily fall upon executive officials. Abuses of power will put the final touch in preparing all institutions for their overthrow and everything will fly skyward under the blows of the maddened mob.

All people are chained down to heavy toil by poverty more firmly than ever they were chained by slavery and serfdom; from these, one way and another, they might free themselves, these could be settled with, but from want they will never get away. We have included in the constitution such rights as to the masses appear fictitious and not actual rights. All these so-called "People's Rights" can exist only in idea, an idea which can never be realized in practical life. What is it to the proletariat labourer, bowed double over his heavy toll, crushed by his lot in life, if talkers get the right to bable, if journalists get the right to scribble any nonsense side by side with good stuff, once the proletariat has no other profit out of the constitution save only those pitiful crumbs which we fling them from our table in return for their voting in favour of what we dictate, in favour of the men we place in power, the servants of our *agentur* . . . . Republican rights for a poor man are no more than a bitter piece of irony, for the necessity he is under of toiling almost all day gives him no present use of them, but on the other hand robs him of all guarantee of regular and certain earnings by making him dependent on strikes by his comrades or lockouts by his masters.

The people under our guidance have annihilated the aristocracy, who were their one and only defence and foster-mother for the sake of their own advantage which is inseparably bound up with the well-being of the people. Nowadays, with the destruction of the aristocracy, the people have fallen into the grips of merciless money-grinding scoundrels who have laid a pitiless and cruel yoke upon the necks of the workers.

We appear on the scene as alleged saviours of the worker from this oppression when we propose to him to enter the ranks of our fighting forces — Socialists, Anarchists, Communists — to whom we always give support in accordance with an alleged brotherly rule (of the solidarity of all humanity) of our *social masonry*. The aristocracy, which enjoyed by law the labour of the workers, was interested in seeing that the workers were well fed, healthy and strong. We are interested in just the opposite — in the deminution, the *killing out ·of the* GOYIM. Our power is in the chronic shortness of food and physical weakness of the worker because by all that this implies he is made the slave of our will, and he will not find in his own authorities either strength or energy to set against our will. Hunger creates the right of capital to rule the worker more surely than it was given to the aristocracy by the legal authority of kings.

By want and the envy and hatred which it engenders we shall move the mobs and with their hands we shall wipe out all those who hinder us on our way.

When the hour strikes for our Sovereign Lord of all the World to be crowned it is these same hands which will sweep away everything that might be a hindrance thereto.

The *goyim* have lost the habit of thinking unless prompted by the suggestions of our specialists. Therefore they do not see the urgent necessity of what we, when our kingdom comes, shall adopt at once, namely this, that *it is essential to teach in national schools one simple, true piece of knowledge, the basis of all knowledge — the knowledge of the structure of human life, of social existence, which requires division of labour, and, consequently, the division of men into classes and conditions.* It is essential for all to know that *owing to difference in the objects of human activity there cannot be any equality,* that he who by any act of his compromises a whole class cannot be equally responsible before the law with him who affects no one but only his own honour. The true knowledge of the structure of society, into the secrets of which we do not admit the *goyim,* would demonstrate to all men that the positions and work must be kept within a certain circle, that they may not become a source of human suffering, arising from an education which does not correspond with the work which individuals are called upon to do. After a thorough study of this knowledge the peoples will voluntarily submit to authority and accept such position as is appointed them in the State. In the present state of knowledge and the direction we have given to its development the people, blindly believing things in print — cherishes — thanks to

promptings intended to mislead and to its own ignorance
—a blind hatred towards all conditions which it considers
above itself, for it has no understanding of the meaning
of class and condition.

This hatred will be still further magnified by the
effects of an *economic crisis,* which will stop dealings
on the exchanges and bring industry to a standstill. We
shall create by all the secret subterranean methods open
to us and with the aid of gold, which is all in our hands,
*a universal economic crisis whereby we shall throw upon
the streets whole mobs of workers simultaneously in all
the countries of Europe.* These mobs will *rush delight-
edly* to shed the blood of those whom, in the simplicity
of their ignorance, they have envied from their cradles,
and whose property they will then be able to loot.

*"Ours" they will not touch, because the moment of
attack will be known to us and we shall take measures
to protect our own.*

We have demonstrated that progress will bring all the
goyim to the sovereignty of reason. Our despotism will
be precisely that; for it will know how by wise severities
to pacificate all unrest, to cauterise liberalism out of all
institutons.

When the populace has seen that all sorts of concessions and indulgences are yielded it in the name of freedom it has imagined itself to be sovereign lord and has
stormed its way to power, but, naturally, like every other
blind man it has come upon a host of stumbling blocks,
*it has rushed to find a guide, it has never had the sense
to return to the former state* and it has laid down its
plenipotentiary powers at *our* feet. Remember the French
Revolution, to which it was we who gave the name of
"Great": the secrets of its preparations are well known
to us for it was wholly the work of our hands.

Ever since that time we have been leading the peoples
from one disenchantment to another, so that in the end
they should turn also from us in favour of that *King-*

Despot of the blood of Zion, whom we are preparing for the world.

At the present day we are, as an international force, invincible, because if attacked by some we are supported by other States. It is the bottomless rascality of the *goyim* peoples, who crawl on their bellies to force, but are merciless towards weakness ,unsparing to faults and indulgent to crimes, unwilling to bear the contradictions of a free social system but patient unto martyrdom under the violence of a bold despotism—it is those qualities which are aiding us to independence. From the premier-dictators of the present day the *goyim* peoples suffer patiently and bear such abuses as for the least of them they would have beheaded twenty kings.

What is the explanation of this phenomenon, this curious inconsequence of the masses of the peoples in their attitude towards what would appear to be events of the same order?

It is explained by the fact that these dictators whisper to the peoples through their agents that through these abuses they are inflicting injury on the States with the highest purpose — to secure the welfare of the peoples, the international brotherhood of them all, their solidarity and equality of rights. Naturally they do not tell the peoples that this unification must be accomplished only under our sovereign rule.

And thus the people condemn the upright and acquit the guilty, persuaded ever more and more that it can do whatsoever it wishes. Thanks to this state of things the people are destroying every kind of stability and creating disorders at every step.

The word "freedom" brings out the communities of men to fight against every kind of force, against every kind of authority, even against God and the laws of nature. For this reason we, when we come into our kingdom, shall have to erase this word from the lexicon of life as implying a principle of brute force which turns mobs into bloodthirsty beasts.

These beasts, it is true, fall asleep again every time when they have drunk their fill of blood, and at such times can easily be riveted into their chains. But if they be not given blood they will not sleep and continue the struggle.

PROTOCOL NO. 4

Stages of a Republic. Gentile Masonry. Freedom and Faith. International Industrial Competition. Role of Speculation. Cult of Gold.

Every republic passes through several stages. The first of these is comprised in the early days of mad raging by the blind mob, tossed hither and thither, right and left: the second is demogogy, from which is born anarchy, and that leads inevitably to despotism—not any longer legal and overt, and therefore responsible despotism, but to unseen and secretly hidden, yet nevertheless sensibly felt despotism in the hands of some secret organization or other, whose acts are the more unscrupulous inasmuch as it works behind a screen, behind the backs of all sorts of agents, the changing of whom not only does not injuriously affect but actually aids the secret force by saving it, thanks to continual changes, from the necessity of expending its resources on the rewarding of long services.

Who and what is in a position to overthrow an invisible force? And this is precisely what our force is. *Gentile* masonry blindly serves as a screen for us and our objects, but the plan of action of our force, even its very abiding-place, remains for the whole people an unknown mystery.

But even freedom might be harmless and have its place in the State economy without injury to the well-being of the peoples if it rested upon the foundation of faith in God, upon the brotherhood of humanity, unconnected with the conception of equality, which is negatived by the very laws of creation, for they have established subordination. With such a faith as this a people might be governed by a wardship of parishes, and would walk contentedly and humbly under the guiding hand of its spiritual pastor submitting to the dispositions of God upon earth. This is the reason why *it is indispensable for us to undermine all faith, to tear of minds out of the* GOYIM *the very principle of Godhead and the spirit, and to put in its place arithmetical calculations and material needs.*

In order to give the *goyim* no time to think and take note, their minds must be diverted towards industry and trade. Thus, all the nations will be swallowed up in the pursuit of gain and in the race for it will not take note of their common foe. But again, in order that freedom may once for all disintegrate and ruin the communities of the *goyim,* we must put industry on a speculative basis: the result of this will be that what is withdrawn from the land by industry will slip through the hands and pass into speculation, that is, to our classes.

The intensified struggle for superiority and shocks delivered to economic life will create, nay, have already created, disenchanted, cold and heartless communities. Such communities will foster a strong aversion towards the higher political and towards religion. Their only guide is gain, that is Gold, which they will erect into a veritable cult, for the sake of those material delights which it can give. Then will the hour strike when, not for the sake of attaining the good, not even to win wealth, but solely out of hatred towards the privileged, the lower classes of the *goyim* will follow our lead against our rivals for power, the intellectuals of the *goyim.*

PROTOCOL NO. 5

Creation of an intensified centralization of government. Methods of seizing power by masonry. Causes of the impossibility of agreement between States. The state of "predestination" of the Jews. Gold — the engine of the machinery of States. Significance of criticism. "Show" institutions. Weariness from word-spinning. How to take a grip of public opinion. Significance of personal initiative. The Super-Government.

What form of administrative rule can be given to communities in which corruption has penetrated everywhere, communities where riches are attained only by the clever surprise tactics of semi-swindling tricks; where looseness reigns: where morality is maintained by penal measures and harsh laws but not by voluntarily accepted principles: where the feelings toward faith and country are obliterated by cosmopolitan convictions? What form of rule is to be given to these commuinties if not that despotism which I shall describe to you later? We shall create an intensified centralization of government in order to grip in or hands all the forces of the community. We shall regulate mechanically all the actions of the political life of our subjects by new laws. These laws will withdraw one by one all the indulgences and liberties which have been permitted by the *goyim,* and our kingdom will be distinguished by a despotism of such magnificent proportions as to be at any moment and in every place in a position to wipe out any *goyim* who oppose us by deed or word.

We shall be told that such a despotism as I speak of is not consistent with the progress of these days, but I will prove to you that it is.

In the times when the peoples looked upon kings on their thrones as on a pure manifestation of the will of God, they submitted without a murmur to the despotic power of kings: but from the day when we insinuated into their minds the conception of their own rights they

began to regard the occupants of thrones as mere ordinary
mortals. The holy unction of the Lord's Anointed has
fallen from the heads of kings in the eye of the people,
and when we also robbed them of their faith in God the
might of power was flung upon the streets into the place
of public proprietorship and was seized by us.

Moreover, the art of directing masses and individuals
by means of cleverly manipulated theory and verbiage, by
regulations of life in common and all sorts of other
quirks, in all which the *goyim* understand nothing, belongs likewise to the specialists of our administrative
brain. Reared on analysis, observation, on delicacies of
fine calculation, in this species of skill we have no rivals,
any more than we have either in the drawing up of plans
of political actions and solidarity. In this respect the
Jesuits alone might have compared with us, but we have
contrived to discredit them in the eyes of the unthinking
mob as an overt organization, while we ourselves all the
while have kept our secret organization in the shade. However, it is probably all the same to the world who is its
sovereign lord, whether the head of Catholicism or our
despot of the blood of Zion! But to us, the Chosen
People, it is very far from being a matter of indifference.

*For a time perhaps we might be successfully dealt with
by a coalition of the* GOYIM *of all the world*: but from
this danger we are secured by the discord existing among
them whose roots are so deeply seated that they can never
now be plucked up. We have set one against another the
personal and national reckonings of the *goyim*, religious
and race hatreds, which we have fostered into a huge
growth in the course of the past twenty centuries. This
is the reason why there is not one State which would
anywhere receive support if it were to raise its arm, for
every one of them must bear in mind that any agreement
against us would be unprofitable to itself. We are too
strong — there is no evading our power. *The nations*

cannot come to even an inconsiderable private agreement without our secretly having a hand in it.

"*Per Me reges regnant*". ("It is through me that Kings reign.") And it was said by the prophets that we were chosen by God Himself to rule over the whole earth. God has endowed us with genius that we may be equal to our task. Were genius in the opposite camp it would still struggle against us, but even so a newcomer is no match for the old-established settler; the struggle would be merciless between us, such a fight as the world has never yet seen. Aye, and the genius on their side would have arrived too late. All the wheels of the machinery of all States go by the force of the engine, which is in our hands, and that engine of the machinery of States is — Gold. The science of political economy invented by our learned elders has for long past been giving royal prestige to capital.

Capital, if it is to co-operate untrammelled, must be free to establish a monopoly of industry and trade: this is already being put in execution by an unseen hand in all quarters of the world. This freedom will give political force to those engaged in industry, and that will help to oppress the people. Nowadays it is more important to disarm the peoples than to lead them into war; more important to use for our advantage the passions which have burst into flames than to quench their fire; more important to catch up and interpret the ideas of others to suit ourselves than to eradicate them. *The principal object of our directorate consists in this: to debilitate the public mind by criticism; to lead it away from serious reflections calculated to arouse resistance; to distract the forces of the mind towards a sham fight of empty eloquence.*

In all ages the peoples of the world, equally with individuals, have accepted words for deeds, for *they are content with a show* and rarely pause to note, in the public arena, whether promises are followed by performance.

Therefore we shall establish show institutions which will give eloquent proof of their benefit to progress.

We shall assume to ourselves the liberal physiognomy of all parties, of all directions, and we shall give that physiognomy a voice *in orators who will speak so much that they will exhaust the patience of their hearers and produce an abhorrence of oratory.*

In order to put public opinion into our hands we must bring it into a state of bewilderment by giving expression from all sides to so many contradictory opinions and for such length of time as will suffice to make the GOYIM *lose their heads in the labyrinth and come to see that the best thing is to have no opinion of any kind in matters political,* which it is not given to the public to understand, because they are understood only by him who guides the public. This is the first secret.

The second secret reqiusite for the success of our government is comprised in the following: To multiply to such an extent national failings, habits, passions, conditions of civil life, that it will be impossible for anyone to know where he is in the resulting chaos, so that the people in consequence will fail to understand one another. This measure will also serve us in another way, namely, to sow discord in all parties, to dislocate all collective forces which are still unwilling to submit to us, and to discourage any kind of personal initiative which might in any degree hinder our affair. *There is nothing more dangerous than personal initiative;* if it has genius behind it, such initiative can do more than can be done by millions of people among whom we have sown discord. We must so direct the education of the *goyim* communities that whenever they come upon a matter requiring initiative they may drop their hands in despairing impotence. The strain which results from freedom of action saps the forces when it meets with the freedom of another. From this collision arise grave moral shocks, disenchantments, failures. *By all these means we shall so wear down the*

GOYIM *that they will be compelled to offer us international power of a nature that by its position will enable us without .any violence gradually to absorb all the State forces of the world and to form a Super-Government.* In place of the rulers of to-day we shall set up a bogey which will be called the Super-Government Administration. Its hands will reach out in all directions like nippers and its organization will be of such colossal dimensions that it cannot fail to subdue all the nations of the world.

PROTOCOL NO. 6

Monopolies; upon them depend the fortunes of the *goyim.* Taking of the land out of the hands of the aristocracy. Trade, Industry and Speculation. Luxury. Rise of wages and increase of price in the articles of primary necessity. Anarchism and drunkeness. Secret meaning of the propaganda of economic theories.

We shall soon begin to establish huge monopolies, reservoirs of colossal riches, upon which even large fortunes of the *goyim* will depend to such an extent that they will go to the bottom together with the credit of the States on the day after the poilical smash . . . .

You gentlemen here present who are economists, just strike an estimate of the significance of this combination!

In every possible way we must develop the significance of our Super-Government by representing it as the Protector and Benefactor of all those who voluntarily submit to us.

The aristocracy of the *goyim* as a political force, is dead — we need not take it into account; but as landed proprietors they can still be harmful to us from the fact that they are self-sufficing in the resources upon which they live. It is essential therefore for us at whatever cost to deprive them of their land. This object will be best attained by increasing the burdens upon landed property

— in loading lands with debt. These measures will check land-holding and keep it in a state of humble and unconditional submission.

The aristocrats of the *goyim*, being hereditarily incapable of contenting themselves with little, will rapidly burn up and fizzle out.

At the same time we must intensively patronize trade and industry, but, first and foremost, speculation, the part played by which is to provide a counterpoise to industry: the absence of speculative industry will multiply capital in private hands and will serve to restore agriculture by freeing the land from indebtedness to the land banks. What we want is that industry should drain off from the land both labour and capital and by means of speculation transfer into our hands all the money of the world, and thereby throw all the *goyim* into the ranks of the proletariat. Then the *goyim* will bow down before us, if for no other reason but to get the right to exist.

To complete the ruin of the industry of the *goyim* we shall bring to the assistance of speculation the luxury which we have developed among the *goyim*, that greedy demand for luxury which is swallowing up everything. *We shall raise the rate of wages which, however, will not bring any advantage to the workers, for at the same time, we shall produce a rise in prices of the first necessaries of life, alleging that it arises from the decline of agriculture and cattle-breeding: we shall further undermine artfully and deeply sources of production, by accustoming the workers to anarchy and to drunkenness and side by side therewith taking all measure to extirpate from the fact of the earth all the educated forces of the GOYIM.*

In order that the true meaning of things may not strike the GOYIM before the proper time we shall mask it under an alleged ardent desire to serve the working classes and the great principles of political economy about which our economic theories are carrying on an energetic propaganda.

PROTOCOL NO. 7

Object of the intensification of armaments. Ferments, discords and hostility all over the world. Checking the opposition of the *goyim* by wars and by a universal war. Secrecy means success in the political. The Press and public opinion. The guns of America, China and Japan.

The intensification of armaments, the increase of police forces — are all essential for the completion of the aforementioned plans. What we have to get at is that there should be in all the States of the world, besides ourselves, only the masses of the proletariat, a few millionaries devoted to our interests, police and soldiers.

Throughout all Europe, and by means of relations with Europe, in other continents also, we must create ferments, discords and hostility. Therein we gain a double advantage. In the first place we keep in check all countries, for they well know that we have the power whenever we like to create disorders or to restore order. All these countries are accustomed to see in us an indispensable force of coercion. In the second place, by our intrigues we shall tangle up all the threads which we have stretched into the cabinets of all States by means of the political, by economic treaties, or loan obligations. In order to succeed in this we must use great cunning and penetration during negotiations and agreements, but, as regards what is called the "official laguage," we shall keep to the opposite tactics and assume the mask of honesty and compliancy. In this way the peoples and governments of the *goyim*, whom we have taughts to look only at the outside whatever we present to their notice, will still continue to accept us as the benefactors and saviours of the human race.

We must be in a position to respond to every act of opposition by war with the neighbours of that country which dares to oppose us: but if these neighbours should also venture to stand collectively together against us, then we must offer resistance by a universal war.

The principal factor of success in the political is the secrecy of its undertakings: the word should not agree with the deeds of the diplomat.

We must compel the governments of the *goyim* to take action in the direction favoured by our widely-conceived plan, already approaching the desired consummation, by what we shall represent as public opiniòn, secretly prompted by us through the means of that so-called "Great Power" — *the Press, which, with a few exceptions that may be disregarded, is already entirely in our hands.*

In a word, to sum up our system of keeping the governments of the *goyim* in Europe in check, we shall show our strength to one of them by terrorist attempts and to all, if we allow the possibility of a general rising against us, we shall respond with the guns of America or China or Japan.

PROTOCOL NO. 8

Ambiguous employment of juridical rights. Assistants of the Masonic directorate. Special schools and super-educational training. Economists and millionaires. To whom to entrust responsible posts in the government.

We must arm ourselves with all the weapons which our opponents might employ against us. We must search out in the very finest shades of expression and the knotty points of the lexicon of law justification for those cases where we shall have to pronounce judgments that might appear abnormally audacious and unjust, for it is important that these resolutions should be set forth in expressions that shall seem to be the most exalted moral principles cast into legal form. Our directorate must surround itself with all these forces of civilization among which it will have to work. It will surround itself with publicists, practical jurists, administrators, diplomats and, finally, with persons prepared by a special super-educational training *in our special schools*. These persons will have cognisance of all the secrets of the social structure, they will know all the languages that can be made up by political alphabets and words; they will be made acquainted with the whole underside of human nature, with all its sensitive chords on which they will have to play. These chords are the cast of mind of the *goyim*, their tendencies, shortcomings, vices and qualities, the particularities of classes and conditions. Needless to say that the talented assistants of authority, of whom I speak, will be taken not from among the *goyim*, who are accustomed to perform their administrative work without giving themselves the trouble to think what its aim is, and never consider what it is needed for. The administrators of the *goyim* sign papers without reading them, and they serve either for mercenary reasons or from ambition.

We shall surround our government with a whole world of economists. That is the reason why economic sciences from the principal subject of the teaching given to the Jews. Around us again will be a whole constellation of bankers, industrialists, capitalists and — *the main thing — millionaires, because in substance everything will be settled by the question of figures.*

For a time, until there will no longer be any risk in entrusting responsible posts in our States to our brother-Jews, we shall put them in the hands of persons whose past and reputation are such that between them and the people lies an abyss, persons who, in case of disobedience to our instructions, must face criminal charges or disappear — this in order to make them defend our interests to their last gasp.

PROTOCOL NO. 9

Application of masonic principles in the matter of re-educating the peoples. Masonic watchword. Meaning of Anti-Semitism. Dictatorship of masonry. Terror. Who are the servants of masonry. Meaning of the "clear-sighted" and the "blind" forces of the *goyim* States. Communion between authority and mob. Licence of liberalism. Seizure of education and training. False theories. Interpretation of laws. The "undergrounds" (*metropolitains*).

In applying our principles let attention be paid to the character of the people in whose country you live and act; a general, identical application of them, until such time as the people shall have been re-educated to our pattern, cannot have success. But by approaching their application cautiously you will see that not a decade will pass before the most stubborn character will change and we shall add a new people to the ranks of those already subdued by us.

The words of the liberal, which are in effect the words of our masonic watchword, namely, "Liberty, Equality, Fraternity," will, when we come into our kingdom, be changed by us into words no longer of a watchword, but only an expression of idealism, namely, into: "The right of liberty, the duty of equality, the ideal of brotherhood." That is how we shall put it, — and so we shall catch the bull by the horns. . . . . . *De facto* we have already wiped out every kind of rule except our own, although *de jure* there still remain a good many of them. Nowadays, if any States raise a protest against us it is only *pro forma* at our discretion and by our direction, for *their anti-Semitism is indispensable to us for the management of our lesser brethren.* I will not enter into further explanations, for this matter has formed the subject of repeated discussions amongst us.

For us there are no checks to limit the range of our activity. Our Super-Government subsists in extra-legal conditions which are described in the accepted terminology by the energetic and forcible word — Dictatorship. I am in a position to tell you with a clear conscience that at the proper time we, the lawgivers, shall execute judgement and sentence, we shall slay and we shall spare, we, as head of all our troops, are mounted on the steed of the leader. We rule by force of will, because in our hands are the fragments of a once powerful party, now vanquished by us. *And the weapons in our hands are limitless ambitions, burning greediness, merciless vengeance, hatreds and malice.*

It is from us that the all-engulfing terror proceeds. We have in our service persons of all opinions, of all doctrines, restorating monarchists, demagogues, socialists, communists, and utopian dreamers of every kind. We have harnessed them all to the task: *each one of them on his own account is boring away at the last remnants of authority, is striving to overthrow all established form of order.* By these acts all States are in torture; they exhort to tranquillity, are ready to sacrifice everything for peace: *but we will not give them peace until they openly acknowledge our international Super-Government,* and with submissiveness.

The people have raised a howl about the necessity of settling the question of Socialism by way of an international agreement. *Division into fractional parties has given them into our hands, for, in order to carry on a contested struggle one must have money, and the money is all in our hands.*

We might have reason to apprehend a union between the "clear-sighted" force of the *goy* kings on their thrones and the *"blind"* force of the *goy* mobs, but we have taken all the needful measure against any such possibility: between the one and the other force we have erected a bulwark in the shape of a mutual terror between them. In

this way the blind force of the people remains our support
and we, and we only, shall provide them with a leader
and, of course, direct them along the road that leads to
our goal.

In order that the hand of the blind mob may not free
itself from our guiding hand, we must every now and
then enter into close communion with it, if not actually
in person, at any rate through some of the most trusty
of our brethren. When we are acknowledged as the only
authority we shall discuss with the people personally on
the market places, and we shall instruct them on questions
of the political in such wise as may turn them in the
direction that suits us.

Who is going to verify what is taught in the village
schools? But what an envoy of the government or a
king on his throne himself may say cannot but become
immediately known to the whole State, for it will be
spread abroad by the voice of the people.

In order not to annihilate the institutions of the *goyim*
before it is time we have touched them with craft and de-
licacy, and have taken hold of the ends of the springs
which move their mechanism. These springs lay in a strict
but just sense of order; we have replaced them by the
chaotic license of liberalism. We have got our hands into
the administration of the law, into the conduct of
elections, into the press, into liberty of the person, *but
principally into education and training as being the cor-
ner-stones of a free existence.*

*We have fooled, bemused and corrupted the youth of
the goyim by rearing them in principles and theories
which are known to us to be false although it is by us
that they have been inculcated.*

Above the existing laws without substantially altering
them, and by merely twisting them into contradictions
of interpertations, we have erected something grandiose
in the way of results. These results found expression first
in the fact that the *interpretations masked the laws*: after-

wards they entirely hid them from the eyes of the governments owing to the impossibility of making anything out of the tangled web of legislation.

This is the origin of the theory of course of arbitration.

You may say that the *goyim* will rise upon us, arms in hand, if they guess what is going on before the time comes; but in the West we have against this a manoeuvre of such appalling terror that the very stoutest hearts quail — the undergrounds, metropolitains, those subterranean corridors which, before the time comes, will be driven under all the capitals and from whence those capitals will be blown into the air with all their organizations and archives.

PROTOCOL NO. 10

The outside appearances in the political. The "genius" of rascality. What is promised by a Masonic *coup d'état?* Universal suffrage. Self-importance. Leaders of Masonry. The genius who is guide of Masonry. Institutions and their functions. The poison of liberalism. Constitution — a school of party discords. Era of republics. Presidents — the puppets of Masonry. Responsibility · of Presidents. "Panama" Part played by chamber of deputies and president. Masonry — the legislative force. New republican constitution. Transition to masonic "despotism." Moment for the proclamation of "The Lord of all the World." Inoculation of diseases and other wiles of Masonry.

To-day I begin with a repetition of what I said before, and *I beg you to bear in mind that governments and peoples are content in the political with outside appearances.* And how, indeed, are the *goyim* to perceive the underlying meaning of things when their representatives give the best of their energies to enjoying themselves? For

Our policy it is of the greatest importance to take cognisance of this detail; it will be of assistance to us when we come to consider the division of authority, freedom of speech, of the press, of religion (faith), of the law of association, of equality before the law, of the inviolability of property, of the dwelling, of taxation (the idea of concealed taxes), of the reflex force of the laws. All these questions are such as ought not to be touched upon directly and openly before the people. In cases where it is indispensable to touch upon them they must not be categorically named, it must merely be declared without detailed exposition that the principles of contemporary law are acknowledged by us. The reason of keeping silence in this respect is that by not naming a principle we leave ourselves freedom of action, to drop this or that out of it without attracting notice; if they were all categorically named they would all appear to have been already given.

The mob cherishes a special affection and respect for the geniuses of political power and accepts all their deeds of violence with the admiring response: "rascally, well, yes, it is rascally, but it's clever!....a trick, if you like, but how craftily played, how magnificently done, what impudent audacity!"....

We count upon attracting all nations to the task of erecting the new fundamental structure, the project for which has been drawn up by us. This is why, before everything, it is indispensable for us to arm ourselves and to store up in ourselves that absolutely reckless audacity and irresistible might of the spirit which in the person of our active workers will break down all hindrances on our way.

When we have accomplished our coup d'état we shall say then to the various peoples: "Everything has gone terribly badly, all have been worn out with sufferings. We are destroying the causes of your torment — nationalities, frontiers, differences of coinages. You are at liberty, of course, to pronounce sentence upon us, but can it pos-

sibly be a just one if it is confirmed by you before you make any trial of what we are offering you." .... *Then will the mob exalt us and bear us up in their hands in a unanimous triumph of hopes and expectations. Voting, which we have made the instrument will set us on the throne of the world by teaching even the very smallest units of members of the human race to vote by means of meetings and agreements by groups, will then have served its purposes and will play its part then for the last time by a unanimity of desire to make close acquaintance with us before condemning us.*

To secure this we must have everybody vote without distinction of classes and qualifications, in order to establish an absolute majority, which cannot be got from the educated propertied classes. In this way, by inculcating in all a sense of self-importance, we shall destroy among the *goyim* the importance of the family and its educational value and remove the possibility of individual minds splitting off, for the mob, handled by us, will not let them come to the front nor even give them a hearing; it is accustomed to listen to us only who pay it for obedience and attention. In this way we shall create a blind, mighty force which will never be in a position to move in any direction without the guidance of our agents set at its head by us as leaders of the mob. The people will submit to this régime because it will know that upon these leaders will depend its earnings, gratifications and the receipt of all kinds of benefits.

A scheme of government should come ready made from one brain, because it will never be clinched firmly if it is allowed to be split into fractional parts in the minds of many. It is allowable, therefore, for us to have cognisance of the scheme of action but not to discuss it lest we disturb its artfulness, the interdependence of its component parts, the practical force of the secret meaning of each clause. To discuss and make alterations in a labor of this kind by means of numerous votings is to impress upon it the stamp of all ratiocinations and mis-understandings which have failed to penetrate the depth and nexus of its plottings. We want our schemes to be forcible and suitably concocted. Therefore WE OUGHT NOT TO FLING THE WORK OF GENIUS OF OUR GUIDE to the fangs of the mob or even of a select company.

These schemes will not turn existing institutions upside down just yet. They will only affect changes in their economy and consequently in the whole combined movement of their progress, which will thus be directed along the paths laid down in our schemes.

Under various names there exists in all countries approximately one and the same thing. Representation, Ministry, Senate, State Council, Legislative and Executive Corps. I need not explain to you the mechanism of the relation of these institutions to one another, because you are aware of all that; only take note of the fact that each of the above-named institutions corresponds to some important function of the State, and I would beg you to remark that the word "important" I apply not to the institution but to the function, consequently it is not the institutions which are important but their functions. These institutions have divided up among themselves all the functions of government — administrative, legislative, executive, wherefore they have come to operate as do the organs in the human body. If we injure one part in the machinery of State, the State falls sick, like a human body, and . . . . . will die.

When we introduced into the State organism the poison of Liberalism its whole political complexion underwent a change. States have been seized with a mortal illness — blood-poisoning. All that remains is to await the end of their death agony.

Liberalism produced Constitutional States, which took the place of what was the only safeguard of the goyim, namely, Despotism; and a constitution, as you well *know, is nothing else but a school of discords,* misunderstandings, quarrels, disagreements, fruitless party agitations, party whims — in a word, a school of everything that serves to destroy the personality of State activity. *The tribune of the "talkeries" has, no less effectively than the Press, condemned the rulers to inactivity and impotence,* and thereby rendered them useless and superflous, for which reason indeed they have been in many countries deposed. *Then it was that the era of republics became possible of realization; and then it was that we replaced the ruler by a caricature of a government — by a president, taken from the mob, from the midst of our puppet creatures, our slaves.* This was the foundation of the mine which we have laid under the *goy* people, I should rather say, under the *goy* peoples.

In the near future we shall establish the responsibility of presidents.

By that time we shall be in a position to disregard forms in carrying through matters for which our impersonal puppet will be responsible. What do we care of the ranks of those striving for power should be thinned, if there should arise a deadlock from the impossibility of finding presidents, a deadlock which will finally disorganize the country? . . . .

In order that our scheme may produce this result we shall arrange elections in favour of such presidents as have in their past some dark, undiscovered stain, some "Panama" or other — then they will be .trustworthy agents for the accomplishment of our plans out of fear of revelations and from the natural desire of everyone who has attained power, namely, the retention of the privileges, advantages and honour connected with the office of president. The chamber of deputies will provide cover for, will protect, will elect presidents, but we shall take from it the right to propose new, or make changes in existing laws, for this right will be given by us to the responsible president, a puppet in our hands. Naturally, the authority of the president will then become a target for every possible form of attack, but we shall provide him with a means of self-defense in the right of an appeal to the people, for the decision of the people over the heads of their representatives, that is to say, an appeal to that same blind slave of ours — the majority of the mob. Independently of this we shall invest the president with the right of declaring a state of war. We shall justify this last right on the ground that the president as chief of the whole army of the country must have it at his disposal, in case of need for the defense of the new republican constitution, the right to defend which will belong to him as the responsible representative of this constitution.

It is easy to understand that in these conditions the key of the shrine will lie in our hands, and no one outside ourselves will any longer direct the force of legislation.

Besides this we shall, with the introduction of the new republican constitution, take from the Chamber the right of interpellation on government measures, on the pretext of preserving political secrecy, and, further, we shall by the new constitution reduce the number of representatives to a minimum, thereby proportionately reducing political passions and the passion for politics. If, however, they should, which is hardly to be expected, burst into flame, even in this minimum, we shall nullify them by a stirring appeal and a reference to the majority of the whole people . . . . . Upon the president will depend the . appointment of presidents and vice-presidents of the Chamber and the Senate. Instead of constant sessions of Parliaments we shall reduce their sittings to a few months. Moreover, the president, as chief of the executive power, will have the right to summon and dissolve Parliament, and, in the latter case, to prolong the time for the appointment of a new parliamentary assembly. But in order that the consequences of all these acts which in substance are illegal, should not, prematurely for our plans, fall upon the responsibility established by us of the president, we *shall instigate ministers and other officials of the higher administration about the president to evade his disposi-tions by taking measures of their own,* for doing which they will be made the scapegoats in his place. . . . This part we especially recommend to be given to be played by the Senate, the Council of State, or the Council of Minis-ters, but not to an individual official.

The president will, at our discretion, interpret the sense of such of the existing laws as admit of various in-terpretation; he will further annul them when we indi-cate to him the necessity to do so, besides this, he will have the right to propose temporary laws, and even new departures in the government constitutional working, the pretext both for the one and the other being the require-ments for the supreme welfare of the State.

By such measures we shall obtain the power of destroy-ing little by little, step by step, all that at the outset when we enter on our rights, we are compelled to introduce into, the constitutions of States to prepare for the transition to an imperceptible abolition of every kind of constitu-tion, and then the time is come to turn every form of government into *our despotism.*

The recognition of our despot may also come before the destruction of the constitution; the moment for this recognition will come when the peoples, utterly wearied by the irregularities and incompetence — a matter which we shall arrange for — of their rulers, will clamour: "Away with them and give us one king over all the earth who will unite us and annihilate the causes of discords — frontiers, nationalities, religions, State debts — who will give us peace and quiet, which we cannot find under our rulers and representatives."

But you yourselves perfectly well know that *to pro-duce the possibility of the expression of such wishes by all the nations it is indispensable to trouble in all countries the people's relations with their governments so as to utterly exhaust humanity with dissension, hatred,*

*struggle, envy and even by the use of torture, by starva-
tion, BY THE INOCULATION OF DISEASES, by
want, so that the* GOYIM *see no other issue than to take
refuge in our complete sovereignty in money and in all
else.*

But if we give the nations of the world a breathing
space the moment we long for is hardly likely ever to
arrive.

PROTOCOL NO. 11

Programme of the new constitution. Certain details of
the proposed revolution. The *goyim* — a pack of
sheep. Secret masonry and its "show" lodges.

The State Council has been, as it were, the emphatic
expression of the authority of the ruler: it will be, as the
"show" part of the Legislative Corps, what may be called
the editorial committee of the laws and decrees of the
ruler.

This, then, is the programme of the new constitution.
We shall make Law, Right and Justice (1) in the guise
of proposals to the Legislative Corps, (2) by decrees of
the president under the guise of general regulations, of
orders of the Senate and of resolutions of the State Council in the guise of ministerial orders, (3) and in case a
suitable occasion should arise — in the form of a revolution in the State.

Having established approximately the *modus agendi*
we will occupy ourselves with details of those combinations by which we have still to complete the revolution
in the course of the machinery of State in the direction
already indicated. By these combinations I mean the
freedom of the Press, the right of association, freedom of
conscience, the voting principle, and many another that
must disappear for ever from the memory of man, or un-
dergo a radical alteration the day after the promulgation

of the new constitution. It is only at that moment that we shall be able at once to announce all our orders, for, afterwards, every noticable alteration will be dangerous, for the following reasons: if this alteration be brought in with harsh severity and in a sense of severity and limitations, it may lead to a feeling of despair caused by fear of new alterations in the same direction; if, on the other hand, it be brought in in a sense of further indulgences it will be said that we have recognized our own wrong-doing and this will destroy the prestige of the infallibility of our authority, or else it will be said that we have become alarmed and are compelled to show a yielding disposition, for which we shall get no thanks because it will be supposed to be compulsory. . . . Both the one and the other are injurious to the prestige of the new constitution. What we want is that from the first moment of its promulgation, while the peoples of the world are still stunned by the accomplished fact of the revolution, still in a condition of terror and uncertainty, they should recognize once for all that we are so strong, so inexpugnable, so superabundantly filled with power, that in no case shall we take any account of them, and so far from paying any attention to their opinions or wishes, we are ready and able to crush with irresistible power all expression or manifestation thereof at every moment and in every place, that we have seized at once everything we wanted and shall in no case divide our power with them. . . . Then in fear and trembling they will close their eyes to everything, and be content to await what will be the end of it all.

The *goyim* are a flock of sheep, and we are their wolves. And you know what happens when the wolves get hold of the flock? . . . .

There is another reason also why they will close their eyes: for we shall keep promising them to give back all the liberties we have taken away as soon as we have quelled the enemies of peace and tamed all parties. . . .

It is not worth while to say anything about how long

a time they will be kept waiting for this return of their liberties. . . .

For what purpose then have we invented this whole policy and insinuated it into the minds of the goys without giving them any chance to examine its underlying meaning? For what, indeed, if not in order to obtain in a roundabout way what is for our scattered tribe unattainable by the direct road? It is this which has served as the basis for our organization of secret masonry which is not known to, and aims which are not even so much as suspected by, these *Goy* cattle, attracted by us into the "Show" army of Masonic Lodges in order to throw dust in the eyes of their fellows.

God has granted to us, His Chosen People, the gift of the dispersion, and in this which appears in all eyes to be our weakness, has come forth all our strength, which has now brought us to the threshold of sovereignty over all the world.

There now remains not much more for us to build up upon the foundation we have laid.

PROTOCOL NO. 12

Masonic interpretation of the word "freedom." Future of the press in the masonic kingdom. Control of the press. Correspondence agencies. What is progress as understood by masonry? More about the press. Masonic solidarity in the press of to-day. The arousing of "public" demands in the provinces. Infallibility of the new régime.

The word "freedom," which can be interpreted in various ways, is defined by us as follows:—

Freedom is the right to do that which the law allows. This interpretation of the word will at the proper time be of service to us, because all freedom will thus be in our hands, since the laws will abolish or create only that which is desirable for us according to the aforesaid programme.

We shall deal with the press in the following way: What is the part played by the press today? It serves to excite and inflame those passions which are needed for our purpose or else it serves selfish ends of parties. It is often vapid, unjust, mendacious, and the majority of the public have not the slightest idea what ends the press really serves. We shall saddle and bridle it with a tight curb: we shall do the same also with all productions of the printing press, for where would be the sense of getting rid of the attacks of the press if we remain targets for pamphlets and books? The produce of publicity, which nowadays is a source of heavy expense owing to the necessity of censoring it, will be turned by us into a very lucrative source of income to our State: we shall lay on it a special stamp tax and require deposits of caution-money before permitting the establishment of any organ of the press or of printing offices; these will then have to guarantee our government against any kind of attack on the part of the press. For any attempt to attack us, if such still be possible, we shall inflict fines without mercy. Such measures as stamp tax, deposits, of caution money and fines secured by these deposits, will bring in a huge income to the government. It is true that party organs might not spare money for the sake of publicity, but these we shall shut up at the second attack upon us. No one shall with impunity lay a finger on the aureole of our government infallibility. The pretext for stopping any publication will be the alleged plea that it is agitating the public mind without occasion or justification. *I beg you to note that among those making attacks upon us will also be organs established by us, but they will attack exclusively points that we have pre-determined to alter.*

Not a single announcement will reach the public without our control. Even now this is already attained by us inasmuch as all news items are received by a few agencies, in whose offices they are focused from all parts of the world. These agencies will then be already entirely ours and will give publicity only to what we dictate to them.

If already now we have contrived to possess ourselves of the minds of the *goy* communities to such an extent that they all come near looking upon the events of the world through the coloured glasses of those spectacles we are setting astride their noses: if already now there is not a single State where there exist for us any barriers to admittance into what *goy* stupidity calls State secrets: what will our position be then, when we shall be acknowledged supreme lords of the world in the person of our king of all the world. . . . .

Let us turn again to the *future of the printing press.* Every one desirous of being a publisher, librarian, or printer, will be obliged to provide himself with the diploma instituted therefor, which, in case of any fault, will be immediately impounded. With such measures *the instrument of thought will become an educative means in the hands of our government, which will no longer allow the mass of the nation to be led astray in by-ways and fantasies about the blessings of progress.* Is there any one of us who does not know that these phantom blessings are the direct roads to foolish imaginings which give birth to anarchical relations of men among themselves and towards authority, because progress, or rather the idea of progress, has introduced the conception of every kind of emancipation, but has failed to establish its limits . . . All the so-called liberals are anarchists, if not in fact, at any rate in thought. Every one of them is hunting after phantoms of freedom, and falling exclusively into license, that is, into the anarchy of protest for the sake of protest.

We turn to the periodical press. We shall impose on it, as on all printed matter, stamp taxes per sheet and deposits of caution-money, and books of less than 30 sheets will pay double. We shall reckon them as pamphlets in order, on the one hand, to reduce the number of magazines, which are the worst form of printed poison, and, on the other, in order that this measure may force writers into such lenghty productions that they will be little read especially as they will be costly. At the same time what we shall publish ourselves to influence mental de- velopment in the direction laid down for our profit will be cheap and will be read voraciously. The tax will bring vapid literary ambitions within bounds and the liability to penalties will make literary men dependent upon us. And if there should be any found who are desirous of writing against us, they will not find any person eager to print their productions. Before accepting any produc- tion for publication in print the publisher or printer will have to apply to the authorities for permission to do so. Thus we shall know beforehand of all tricks preparing against us and shall nullify them by getting ahead with explanations on the subject treated of.

Literature and journalism are two of the most impor- tant educative forces, and therefore our government will become proprietor of the majority of the journals. This will neutralize the injurious influence of the privately- owned press and will put us in possession of the tre- mendous influence upon the public mind. . . . If we give permit for ten journals, we shall ourselves found thirty, and so on the same proportion. This, however, must in nowise be suspected by the public. For which reason all journals published by us will be of the most opposite, in appearance, tendencies and opinions, thereby creating confidence in us and bringing over to us our quite un- suspicious opponents, who will thus fall into our trap and be rendered harmless.

In the front rank will stand organs of an official character. They will always stand guard over our in- terests, and therefore their influence will comparatively insignificant.

In the second rank will be the semi-official organs, whose part it will be to attract the tepid and indifferent.

In the third rank we shall set up our own, to all appearance, opposition, which, in at least one of its organs, will present what looks like the very antipodes to us. Our real opponents at heart will accept this simulated opposition as their own and will show us their cards.

All our newspapers will be of all possible complexions — aristocratic, republican, revolutionary, even anarchical —for so long, of course, as the constitution exists . . . . Like the Indian idol Vishnu they will have a hundred hands, and every one of them will have a finger on any one of the public opinions as required. When a pulse quickens these hands will lead opinion in the direction of our aims, for an excited patient loses all power of judgment and easily yields to suggestion. Those fools who will think they are repeating the opinion of a newspaper of their own camp will be repeating our opinion or any opinion that seems desirable for us. In the vain belief that they are following the organ of their party they will in fact follow the flag which we hang out for them.

In order to direct our newspaper militia in this sense we must take especial and minute care in organizing this matter. Under the title of central department of the press we shall institute literary gatherings at which our agents will without attracting attention issue the orders and watchwords of the day. By discussing and controverting, but always superficially, without touching the essence of the matter, our organs will carry on a sham fight fusillade with the official newspapers solely for the purpose of giving occasion for us to express ourselves more fully than could well be done from the outset in official announcements, whenever, of course, that is to our advantage.

These attacks upon us will also serve another purpose, namely, that our subjects will be convinced of the existence of full freedom of speech and so give our agents an occasion to affirm that all organs which oppose us are empty babblers, since they are incapable of finding any substantial objections to our orders.

Methods of organization like these, imperceptible to the public eye but absolutely sure, are the best calculated to succeed in bringing the attention and the confidence of the public to the side of our government. Thanks to such methods we shall be in a position as from time to time may be required, to excite or to tranquillise the public mind on political questions, to persuade or to confuse, printing now truth, now lies, facts or their contradictions, according as they may be well or ill received, always very cautiously feeling our ground before stepping upon it . . . *We shall have a sure triumph over our opponents since they will not have at their disposition organs of the press in which they can give full and final expression to their views* owing to the aforesaid methods of dealing with the press. We shall not even need to refute them except very superficially.

Trial shots like these, fired by us in the third rank of our press, in case of need, will be energetically refuted by us in our semi-official organs.

Even nowadays, already, to take only the French press, there are forms which reveal masonic solidarity in acting on the watchword: all organs of the press are bound together by professional secrecy; like the augurs of old, not one of their numbers will give away the secret of his sources of information unless it be resolved to make announcement of them. Not one journalist will venture to betray this secret, for not one of them is ever admitted to practise literature unless his whole past has some disgraceful sore or other. . . . . These sores would be immediately revealed. So long as they remain the secret of a few the prestige of the journalist attracts the majority of the country — the mob follow after him with enthusiasm.

Our calculations are especially extended to the provinces. It is indispensable for us to inflame there those hopes and impulses with which we could at any moment fall upon the capital, and we shall represent to the capitals that these expressions are the independent hopes and impulses of the provinces. Naturally, the source of them will be always one and the same — ours. *What we need is that, until such time as we are in the plenitude of power, the capitals should find themselves stifled by the provincial opinion of the nation*, i.e., *of a majority arranged by our agentur.* What we need is that at the psychological moment the capitals should not be in a position to discuss an accomplished fact for the simple reason, if for no other, that it has been accepted by the public opinion of a majority in the provinces.

When we are in the period of the new régime transitional to that of our assumption of full sovereignty we must not admit any revelations by the press of any form of public dishonesty; it is necessary that the new régime should be thought to have so perfectly contented everybody that even criminality has disappeared . . . . Cases of the manifestation of criminality should remain known only to their victims and to chance witnesses — no more.

PROTOCOL NO. 13

The need for daily bread. Questions of the Political. Questions of industry. Amusements. People's Palaces. "Truth is One." The great problems.

The need for daily bread forces the *goyim* to keep silence and be our humble servants. Agents taken on to our press from among the goyim will at our orders discuss anything which it is inconvenient for us to issue directly in official documents, and we meanwhile, quietly amid the din of the discussion so raised, shall simply take and carry through such measures as we wish and then offer them to the public as an accomplished fact. No one will dare to demand the abrogation of a matter once settled, all the more so as it will be represented as an improvement. . . . . . And immediately the press will distract the current of thought towards new questions (have we not trained people always to be seeking something new?). Into the discussions of these new questions will throw themselves those of the brainless dispensers of fortunes who are not able even now to understand that they have not the remotest conception about the matters which they undertake to discuss. Questions of the political are unattainable for any save those who have guided it already for many ages, the creators.

From all this you will see that in securing the opinion of the mob we are only facilitating the working of our machinery, and you may remark that it is not for actions but for words issued by us on this or that question that we seem to seek approval. We are constantly making public declaration that we are guided in all our undertakings by the hope, joined to the conviction, that we are serving the common weal.

In order to distract people who may be too troublesome from discussions of questions of the political we are now putting forward what we allege to be new questions of the political, namely, questions of industry. In this sphere let them discuss themselves silly! The masses are agreed to remain inactive, to take a rest from what they suppose to be political activity (which we trained them to in order to use them as a means of combating the *goy* governments) only on condition of being found new employments, in which we are prescribing them something that looks like the same political object. In order that the masses themselves may not guess what they are about *we further distract them with amusements, games, pastimes, passions, people's palaces. . . Soon we shall begin through the press to propose competitions in art, in sport of all kinds*: these interests will finally distract their minds from question in which we should find ourselves compelled to oppose them. Growing more and more disaccustomed to reflect and form any opinions of their own, people will begin to talk in the same tone as we, because we alone shall be offering them new directions for thought . . . . of course through such persons as will not be suspected of solidarity with us.

The part played by the liberals, utopian dreamers, will be finally played out when our government is acknowledged. Till such time they will continue to do us good service. Therefore we shall continue to direct their minds to all sorts of vain conceptions of fantastic theories, new and apparently progressive: for have we not with complete success turned the brainless heads of the *goyim* with progress, till there it not among the *goyim* one mind able to perceive that under this work lies a departure from truth in all cases where it is not a question of material inventions, for truth is one, and in it there is no place for progress. Progress, like a fallacious idea, serves to obscure truth so that none may know it except us, the Chosen of God, its guardians.

When we come into our kingdom our orators will expound great problems which have turned humanity upside down in order to bring it at the end under our beneficent rule.

Who will ever suspect then that *all these peoples were stage-managed by us according to political plan which no one has so much as guessed at in the course of many centuries?* . . . .

PROTOCOL NO. 14

The religion of the future. Future conditions of serfdom. Inaccessibility of knowledge regarding the religion of the future. Pornography and the printed matter of the future.

When we come into our kingdom it will be undesirable for us that there should exist any other religion than ours of the One God with whom our destiny is bound up by our position as the Chosen People and through whom our same destiny is united with the destinies of the world. We must therefore sweep away all other forms of belief. If this gives birth to the atheists whom we see to-day, it will not, being only a transitional stage, interfere with our views, but will serve as a warning for those generations which will hearken to our preaching of the religion of Moses, that, by its stable and thoroughly elaborated system has brought all the peoples of the world into subjection to us. Therein we shall emphasize its mystical right, on which, as we shall say, all its educative power is based. . . . . Then at every possible opportunity we shall publish articles in which we shall make comparisons between our beneficent rule and those of past ages. The blessings of tranquillity, though it be a tranquillity forcibly brought about by centuries of agitation, will throw into higher relief the benefits to which we shall point. The errors of the *goyim* governments will be depicted by us in the most vivid hues. We shall implant such an abhorrence of them that the peoples will prefer tranquillity in a state of serfdom to those rights of vaunted freedom which have tortured humanity and exhausted the very sources of human existence, sources which have been exploited by a mob of rascally adventurers who know not what they do. . . . *Useless changes of forms of government to which we instigated the* GOYIM *when we were undermining their state structures, will have so wearied the peoples by that time that they will prefer to suffer anything under us rather than run the risk of enduring again all the agitations and miseries they have gone through.*

At the same time we shall not omit to emphasize the historical mistakes of the *goy* governments which have tormented humanity for so many centuries by their lack of understanding of everything that constitutes the true good of humanity in their chase after fantastic schemes of social blessings, and have never noticed that these schemes kept on producing a worse and never a better state of the universal relations which are the basis of human life.. . .

The whole force of our principles and methods will lie in the fact that we shall present them and expound them as a splendid contrast to the dead and decomposed old order of things in social life.

Our philsosophers will discuss all the shortcomings of the various beliefs of the GOYIM, *but no one will ever bring under discussion our faith from its true point of view since this will be fully learned by none save ours, who will never dare to betray its secrets.*

In countries known as progressive and enlightened we have created a senseless, filthy, abominable literature. For some time after our entrance to power we shall continue to encourage its existence in order to provide a telling relief by contrast to the speeches, party programme, which will be distributed from exalted quarters of ours.. . . Our wise men, trained to become leaders of the *goyim,* will compose speeches, projects, memoirs, articles, which will be used by us to influence the minds of the *goyim,* directing them towards such understanding and forms of knowledge as have been determined by us.

PROTOCOL NO. 15

One-day *coup d'état* (revolution) over all the world. Executions. Future lot of *goyim*-masons. Mysticism of authority. Multiplication of masonic lodges. Central governing board of masonic elders. The "Azev-tactics." Masonry as leader and guide of all secret societies. Significance of public applause. Collectivism. Victims. Executions of masons. Fall of the prestige of laws and authority. Our position as the Chosen people. Brevity and clarity of the laws of the kingdom of the future.

Obedience to orders. Measures against abuse of authority. Severity of penalties. Age-limit for judges. Liberalism of judges and authorities. The money of all the world. Absolutism of masonry. Right of appeal. Patriarchal "outside appearance" of the power of the future "ruler." Apotheosis of the ruler. The right of the strong as the one and only right. The King of Israel. Patriarch of all the world.

When we at last definitely come into our kingdom by the aid of *coups détat* prepared everywhere for one and the same day, after the worthlessness of all existing forms of government has been definitely acknowledged (and not a little time will pass before that comes about, perhaps even a whole century) we shall make it our task to see that against us such things as plots shall no longer exist. With this purpose we shall slay without mercy all who take arms (in hand) to oppose our coming into our kingdom. Every kind of new institution of anything like a secret society will also be punished with death; those of them which are now in existence, are known to us, serve us and have served us, we shall disband and send into exile to continents far removed from Europe. *In this way we shall proceed with those* GOY *masons who know too much;* such of these as we may for some reason spare will be kept in constant fear of exile. We shall promulgate a law making all former members of secret societies liable to exile from Europe as the centre of our rule.

Resolutions of our government will be final, without appeal.

In the *goy* societies, in which we have planted and deeply rooted discord and protestantism, the only possible way of restoring order is to employ merciless measures that prove the direct force of authority: no regard must be paid to the victims who fall, they suffer for the well-being of the future. The attainment of that well-being, even at the expense of sacrifices, is the duty of any kind of government that acknowledges as justification for its existence not only its privileges but its obligations. The principal guarantee of stability of rule is to confirm the aureole of power, and this aureole is attained only by such a majestic inflexibility of might as shall carry on its face the emblems of inviolability from mystical causes — from the choice of God. *Such was, until recent times, the Russian autocracy, the one and only serious foe we had in the world, without counting the Papacy.* Bear in mind the example when Italy, drenched with blood, never touched a hair of the head of Sulla who had poured forth that blood: Sulla enjoyed an apotheosis for his might in the eyes of the people, though they had been torn in pieces by him, but his intrepid return to Italy ringed him round with inviolability. The people do not lay a finger on him who hypnotizes them by his daring and strength of mind.

Meantime, however, until we come into our kingdom, we shall act in the contrary way: we shall create and multiply free masonic lodges in all the countries of the world, absorb into them all who may become or who are prominent in public activity, for in these lodges we shall find our principal intelligence office and means of influence. All these lodges we shall bring under one central administration, known to us alone and to all others absolutely unknown, which will be composed of our learned elders. The lodges will have their representatives who will serve to screen the above-mentioned administration of *masonry* and from whom will issue the watchword and programme. In these lodges we shall tie together the knot which binds together all revolutionary and liberal elements. Their composition will be made up of all strata of society. The most secret political plots will be known to us and will fall under our guiding hands on the very day of their conception. *Among the members of these lodges will be almost all the agents of international and national police* since their service is for us irreplaceable in the respect that the police is in a position not only to use its own particular measures with the insubordinate, but also to screen our activities and provide pretexts for discontents, *et cetera*.

The class of people who most willingly enter into secret societies are those who live by their wits, careerists, and in general people, mostly light-minded, with whom we shall have no difficulty in dealing and in using to wind up the mechanism of the machine devised by us. If this world grows agitated the meaning of that will be that we have had to stir it up in order to break up its too great solidarity. *But if there should arise in its midst a plot, then at the head of that plot will be no other than one of our most trusted servants.* It is natural that we and no other should lead *masonic* activities, for we know whither we are leading, we know the final goal of every form of activity whereas the *goyim* have knowledge of nothing, not even of the immediate effect of action; they put before themselves, usually, the momentary reckoning of the satisfaction of their self-opinion in the accomplishment of their thought without even remarking that the very conception never belonged to their initiative but to our instigation of their thought. . . . .

The goyim enter the lodges out of curiosity or in the hope by their means to get a nibble at the public pie, and some of them in order to obtain a hearing before the public for their impracticable and groundless fantasies: they thirst for the emotion of success and applause, of which we are remarkably generous. And the reason why we give them this success is to make use of the high conceit of themselves to which it gives birth, for that insensibly disposes them to assimilate our suggestions without being on their guard against them in the fullness of their confidence that it is their own infallibility which is giving utterance to their own thoughts and that it is impossible for them to borrow those of others. . . . . You cannot imagine to what extent the wisest of the *goyim* can be brought to a state of unconscious naiveté in the presence of this condition of high conceit of themselves, and at the same time how easy it is to take the heart out of them by the slightest ill-success, though it be nothing more than the stoppage of the applause they had, and to reduce them to a slavish submission for the sake of winning a renewal of success. . . . . *By so much as ours disregard success if only they can carry through their plans, by so much the* GOYIM *are willing to sacrifice any plans only to have success.* This psychology of theirs materially facilitates for us the task of setting them in the required direction. These tigers in appearance have the souls of sheep and the wind blows freely through their heads. We have set them on the hobby-horse of an idea about the absorption of individuality by the symbolic unit of *collectivism.*

They have never yet and they never will have the sense to reflect that this hobby-horse is a manifest violation of the most important law of nature, which has established from the very creation of the world one unit unlike another and precisely for the purpose of instituting individuality. . . . .

If we have been able to bring them to such a pitch of stupid blindness is it not a proof, and an amazingly clear proof, of the degree to which the mind of the *goyim* is undeveloped in comparison with our mind? This it is, mainly, which guarantees our success.

And how far-seeing were our learned elders in ancient times when they said that to attain a serious end it behooves not to stop at any means or to count the victims sacrificed for the sake of that end. . . We have not counted the victims of the seed of the goy cattle, though we have sacrificed many of our own, but for that we have now already given them such a position on the earth as they could not even have dreamed of. The comparatively small numbers of the victims from the number of ours have preserved our nationality from destruction.

Death is the inevitable end for all. It is better to bring that end nearer to those who hinder our affairs than to ourselves, to the founders of this affair. *We execute masons in such wise that none save the brotherhood can ever have a suspicion of it, not even the victims themselves of our death sentence, they all die when required as if from a normal kind of illness.* .... Knowing this, even the brotherhood in its turn dare not protest. By such methods we have plucked out of the midst of *masonry* the very root of protest against our disposition. While preaching liberalism to the *goyim* we at the same time keep our own people and our agents in a state of unquestioning submission.

Under our influence the execution of the laws of the *goyim* has been reduced to a minimum. The prestige of the law has been exploded by the liberal interpretations introduced into this sphere. In the most important and fundamental affairs and questions judges decide as we dictate to them, see matters in the light wherewith we enfold them for the administration of the *goyim,* of course, through persons who are our tools though we do not appear to have anything in common with them — by newspaper opinion or by other means. .... Even senators and the higher administration accept our counsels. The purely brute mind of the *goyim* is incapable of use for analysis and observation, and still more for the foreseeing whither a certain manner of setting a question may tend.

In this difference in capacity for thought between the *goyim* and ourselves may be clearly discerned the seal of our position on the Chosen People and of our higher quality of humanness, in contradistinction to the brute mind of the *goyim*. Their eyes are open, but see nothing before them and do not invent (unless, perhaps, material things). From this it is plain that nature herself has destined us to guide and rule the world.

When comes the time of our overt rule, the time to manifest its blessings, we shall remake all legislatures, all our laws will be brief, plain, stable, without any kind of interpretations, so that anyone will be in a position to know them perfectly. The main feature which will run right through them is submission to orders, and this principle will be carried to a grandiose height. Every abuse will then disappear in consequence of the responsibility of all down to the lowest unit before the higher authority of the representative of power. Abuses of power subordinate to this last instance will be so mercilessly punished that none will be found anxious to try experiments with their own powers. We shall follow up jealously every action of the administration on which depends the smooth running of the machinery of the State, for slackness in this produces slackness everywhere; not a single case of illegality or abuse of power will be left without exemplary punishment.

Concealment of guilt, connivance between those in the service of the administration — all this kind of evil will disappear after the very first examples of severe punishment. The aureole of our power demands suitable, that is, cruel, punishments for the slightest infringement, for the sake of gain, of its supreme prestige. The sufferer, though his punishment may exceed his fault, will count as a soldier falling on the administrative field of battle in the interest of authority, principle and law, which do not permit that any of those who hold the reins of the public coach should turn aside from the public highway to their own private paths. *For example: our judges will know that whenever they feel disposed to plume themselves on foolish clemency they are violating the law of justice which is instituted for the exemplary edification of men by penalties for lapses and not for display of the spiritual qualities of the judge . . . .* Such qualities it is proper to show in private life, but not in a public square which is the educationary basis of human life.

Our legal staff will serve not beyond the age of 55, firstly because old men more obstinately hold to prejudiced opinions, and are less capable of submitting to new directions, and secondly because this will give us the possibility by this measure of securing elasticity in the changing of staff, which will thus the more easily bend under our pressure: he who wishes to keep his place will have to give blind obedience to deserve it. In general, our judges will be elected by us only from among those who thoroughly understand that the part they have to play is to punish and apply laws and not to dream about the manifestations of liberalism at the expense of the educationary scheme of the State, as the *goyim* in these days imagine it to be. . . . . This method of shuffling the staff will serve also to explode any collective solidarity of those in the same service and will bind all to the interests of the government upon which their fate will depend. The young generation of judges will be trained in certain views regarding the inadmissibility of any abuses that might disturb the established order of our subjects among themselves.

In these days the judges of the *goyim* create indulgences to every kind of crimes, not having a just understanding of their office, because the rulers of the present age in appointing judges to office take no care to inculcate in them a sense of duty and consciousness of the matetr which is demanded of them. As a brute beast lets out its young in search of prey, so do the *goyim* give their subjects places of profit without thinking to make clear to them for what purpose such place was created. This is the reason why their governments are being ruined by their own forces through the acts of their own administration.

Let us borrow from the example of the results of these actions yet another lesson for our government.

We shall root out liberalism from all the important strategic posts of our government on which depends the training of subordinates for our State structure. Such posts will fall exclusively to those who have been trained by us for administrative rule. To the possible objection that the retirement of old servants will cost the Treasury heavily, I reply, firstly, they will be provided with some private service in place of what they lose, and, secondly, I have to remark that all the money in the world will be concentrated in our hands, consequently it is not our government that has to fear expense.

Our absolutism will in all things be logically consecutive and therefore in each one of its decrees our supreme will will be respected and unquestionably fulfilled: it will ignore all murmurs, all discontents of every kind and will destroy to the root every kind of manifestation of them in act by punishment of an exemplary character.

We shall abolish the right of cassation, which will be transferred exclusively to our dispotal—to the cognisanze of him who rules, for we must not allow the conception among the people of a thought that there could be such a thing as a decision that is not right of judges set up by us. If, however, anything like this should occur, we shall ourselves cassate the decision, but inflict therewith such exemplary punishment on the judge for lack of understanding of his duty and the purpose of his appointment as will prevent a repetition of such cases. . . . . I repeat that it must be borne in mind that we shall know every step of our administration which only needs to be closely watched for 'the people to be content with us, for it has the right to demand from a good government a good official.

Our government will have the appearance of a patriarchial paternal guardianship on the part of our ruler. Our own nation and our subjects will discern in his person a father caring for their every need, their every act, their every inter-relation as subjects one with another, as well as their relations to the ruler. They will then be so thoroughly imbued with the thought that it is impossible for them to dispense with this wardship and guidance, if the wish to live in piece and quiet, *that they will acknowledge the autocracy of our ruler with a devotion bordering on APOTHEOSIS,* especially when they are convinced that those whom we set up do not put their own in place of his authority, but only blindly execute his dictates. They will be rejoiced that we have regulated everything in their lives as is done by wise parents who desire to train their children in the cause of duty and submission. For the peoples of the world in regard to the secrets of our polity are ever through the ages only children under age, precisely as are also their governments.

As you see, I found our despotism on right and duty: the right to compel the execution of duty is the direct obligation of a government which is a father for its subjects. It has the right of the strong that it may use it for the benefit of directing humanity towards that order which is defined by nature, namely, submission. Everything in the world is in a state of submission, if not to man, then to circumstances or its own inner character, in all cases, to what is stronger. And so shall we be this something stronger for the sake of good.

We are obliged without hestitation to sacrifice individuals, who commit a breach of established order, for in the exemplary punishment of evil lies a great educational problem.

When the King of Israel sets upon his sacred head the crown offered him by Europe he will become patriarch of the world. The indispensable victims offered by him in consequence of their suitability will never reach the number of victims offered in the course of conturies by the mania of magnificence, the emulation between the *goy* governments. . .

Our King will be in constant communion with the peoples, making to them from the tribune speeches which fame will in that same hour distribute over all the world.

PROTOCOL NO. 16

Emasculation of the universities. Substitute for classicism. Training and calling. Advertisement of the authority of "the ruler" in the schools. Abolition of freedom of instruction. New Theories. Independence of thought. Teaching by object lessons.

In order to effect the destruction of all collective forces except ours we shall emasculate the first stage of collectivism — the *universities,* by re-educating them in a new direction. *Their officials and professors will be prepared for their business by detailed secret programmes of action from which they will not with immunity diverge, not by one iota. They will be appointed with especial precaution, and will be so placed as to be wholly dependent upon the Government.*

We shall exclude from the course of instruction State Law as also all that concerns the political question. These subjects will be taught to a few dozens of persons chosen for their pre-eminent capacities from among the number of the initiated. *The universities must no longer send out from their halls milksops concocting plans for a constitution, like a comedy or a tragedy, busying themselves with questions of policy in which even their own fathers never had any power of thought.*

The ill-guided acquaintance of a large number of persons with questions of polity creates utopian dreamers and bad subjects, as you can see for yourselves from the example of the universal education in this direction of the *goyim.* We must introduce into their education all those principles which have so brilliantly broken up their order. But when we are in power we shall remove every kind of disturbing subject from the course of education and shall make out of the youth obedient children of authority, loving him who rules as the support and hope of peace and quiet.

Classicism, as also any form of study of ancient history, in which there are more bad than good examples, we shall replace with the study of the programme of the future. We shall erase from the memory of men all facts of previous centuries which are undesirable to us, and leave only those which depict all the errors of the governments of the *goyim*. The study of practical life, of the obligations of order, of the relations of people one to another, of avoiding bad and selfish examples which spread the infection of evil, and similar questions of an educative nature, will stand in the forefront of the teaching programme, which will be drawn up on a separate plan for each calling or state of life, in no wise generalising the teaching. This treatment of the question has special importance.

Each state of life must be trained within strict limits corresponding to its destination and work in life. The *occasional genius has always managed and always will manage to slip through into other states of life, but it is the most perfect folly for the sake of this rare occasional genius to let through into ranks foreign to them the untalented who thus rob of their places those who belong to those ranks by birth or employment. You know yourselves in what all this has ended for the goyim who allowed this crying absurdity.*

In order that he who rules may be seated firmly in the hearts and minds of his subjects it is necessary for the time of his activity to instruct the whole nation in the schools and on the market places about his meaning and his acts and all his beneficent initiatives.

We shall abolish every kind of freedom of instruction. Learners of all ages will have the right to assemble together with their parents in the educational establishments as it were in a club: during these assemblies, on holydays, teachers will read what will pass as free lectures on questions of human relations, of the laws of examples, of the limitations which are born of unconscious relations, and, finally, of the philosophy of new theories not yet declared to the world. These theories will be raised by us to the stage of a dogma of faith as a transitional stage towards our faith. On the completion of this exposition of our programme of action in the present and the future I will read you the principles of these theories.

In a word, knowing by the experience of many centuries that people live and are guided by ideas, that these ideas are imbibed by people only by the aid of education provided with equal success for all ages of growth, but of course by varying methods, we shall swallow up and confiscate to our own use the last scintilla of independence of thought, which we have for long past been directing towards subjects and ideas useful for us. The system of bridling thought is already at work in the so-called system of teaching by *object lessons,* the purpose of which is to turn the *goyim* into unthinking submissive brutes waiting for things to be presented before their eyes in order to form an idea of them. . . In France, one of four best agents, Bourgeois, has already made public a new programme of teaching by object lessons.

PROTOCOL NO. 17

Advocacy. Influence of the priesthood of the *goyim.* Freedom of conscience. Papal Court. King of the Jews as Patriarch-Pope. How to fight the existing Church. Function of contemporary press. Organization of· police. Volunteer police. Espionage on the pattern of the *kabal* espionage. Abuses of authority.

The practice of advocacy produces men cold, cruel, persistent, unprincipled, who in all cases take up an impersonal purely legal standpoint. They have the inveterate habit to refer everything to its value for the defence, not to the public welfare of its results. They do not usually decline to undertake any defence whatever, they strive for an acquittal at all costs, cavilling over every petty crux of jurisprudence and thereby they demoralize justice. For this reason we shall set this profession into narrow frames which will keep it inside this sphere of executive public service. Advocates, equally with judges, will be deprived of the right of communication with litigants; they will receive business only from the court and will study it by notes off report and documents, defending their clients after they have been interrogated in court on facts that have appeared. They will receive an honorarium without regard to the quality of the defence. This will render them mere reporters on law-business in the interests of justice and as counterpoise to the proctor who will be the reporter in the interests of prosecution; this will shorten business before the courts. In this way will be established a practice of honest unprejudiced defence conducted not from personal interest but by conviction. This will also, by the way, remove the present practice of corrupt bargain between advocates to agree only to let that side win which pays most. . . .

We have long past taken care to discredit the priesthood of the goyim, and thereby to ruin their mission on earth which in these days might still be a great hindrance to us. Day by day its influence on the peoples of the world is falling lower. *Freedom of conscience* has been declared everywhere, *so that now only years divide us from the moment of the complete wrecking of that Christian religion,* as to other religions we shall have still less difficulty in dealing with them, but it would be premature to speak of this now. We shall set clericalism and clericals into such narrow frames as to make their influence move in retrogressive proportion to its former progress.

When the time comes finally to destroy the papal court the finger of an invisible hand will point the nations towards this court. When, however, the nations fling themselves upon it, we shall come forward in the guise of its defenders as if to save excessive bloodshed. By this diversion we shall penetrate to its very bowels and be sure we shall never come out again until we have gnawed through the entire strength of this place.

The King of the Jews will be the real Pope of the Universe, the patriarch of an international Church.

But, *in the meantime,* while we are re-educating youth in new traditional religions and afterwards in ours, *we shall not overtly lay a finger on existing churches, but we shall fight against them by criticism calculated to produce schism.* . . . .

In general, then, our contemporary press will continue to *convict* State affairs, religions, incapacities of the *goyim,* always using the most unprincipled expressions in order by every means to lower their prestige in the manner which can only be practiced by the genius of our gifted tribe. . . . .

Our kingdom will be an apologia of the divinity Vishnu, in whom is found its personification — in our hundred hands will be, one in each, the springs of the machinery of social life. We shall see everything without the aid of official police which, in that scope of its rights which we elaborated for the use of the *goyim,* hinders governments from seeing. In our programme *one-third of our subjects will keep the rest under observation* from a sense of duty, on the principle of volunteer service to the State. It will then be no disgrace to be a spy and informer, but a merit: unfounded denunciations, however, will be cruelly punished that there may be no development of abuses of this right.

Our agents will be taken from the higher as well as the lower ranks of society, from among the administrative class who spend their time in amusements, editors, printers and publishers, booksellers, clerks, and salesmen, workmen, coachmen, lackeys, etcetera. This body, having no rights and not being empowered to take any action on their own account, and consequently a police without any power, will only witness and report: verification of their reports and arrests will depend upon a responsible group of controllers of police affairs, while the actual act of arrest will be performed by the gendarmerie and the municipal police. Any person not denouncing anything seen or heard concerning questions of polity will also be charged with and made responsible for concealment, if it be proved that he is guilty of this crime.

Just as nowadays our brethren are obliged at their own risk to denounce to the kabal apostates of their own family or members who have been noticed doing anything in opposition to the kabal, so in our kingdom over all the world it will be obligatory for all our subjects to observe the duty of service to the State in this direction.

Such an organization will extirpate abuses of authority, of force, of bribery, everything in fact which we by our counsels, by our theories of the superhuman rights of man, have introduced into the customs of the *goyim.* . . . But how else were we to procure that increase of causes predisposing to disorders in the midst of their administration? . . . . Among the number of those methods one of the most important is — agents for the restoration of order, so placed as to have the opportunity in their disintegrating activity of developing and displaying their evil enclinations — obstinate self-conceit, irresponsible exercise of authority, and, first and foremost, venality.

PROTOCOL NO. 18

Measures of secret defense. Observation of conspiracies from the inside. Overt secret defense — the ruin of authority. Secret defense of the King of the Jews. Mystical prestige of authority. Arrest on the first suspicion.

When it becomes necessary for us to strengthen the strict measures of secret defense (the most fatal poison for the prestige of authority) we shall arrange a simulation of disorders or some manifestation of discontents finding expression through the co-operation of good speakers. Round these speakers will assemble all who are sympathetic to his utterances. This will give us the pretext for domiciliary perquisitions and surveillance on the part of our servants from among the number of the *goyim* *police*. . . . . .

As the majority of conspirators act out of love for the game, for the sake of talking, so, until they commit some overt act we shall not lay a finger on them but only introduce into their midst observation elements. . . . . It must be remembered that the prestige of authority is lessened if it frequently discovers conspiracies against itself: this implies a presumption of consciousness of weakness, or, what is still worse, of injustice. You are aware that we have broken the prestige of the *goy* kings by frequent attempts upon their lives through our agents, blind sheep of our flock, who are easily moved by a few liberal phrases to crimes provided only they be painted in political colours. *We have compelled the rulers to acknowledge their weakness in advertising overt measures of secret defence and thereby we shall bring the promise of authority to destruction.*

Our ruler will be secretly protected only by the most insignificant guard, because we shall not admit so much as a thought that there could exist against him any sedition with which he is not strong enough to contend and is compelled to hide from it.

If we should admit this thought, as the *goyim* have done and are doing, we should *ipso facto* be signing a death sentence, if not for our ruler, at any rate for his dynasty, at no distant date.

According to strictly enforced outward appearances our ruler will employ his power only for the advantage of the nation and in no wise for his own or dynastic profits. Therefore, with the observance of this decorum, his authority will be respected and guarded by the subjects themselves, it will receive an apotheosis in the admission that with it is bound up the well-being of every citizen of the State, for upon it will depend all order in the common life of the pack. . . . .

Overt defense of the kind argues weakness in the organization of his strength.

Our ruler will always among the people be surrounded by a mob of apparently curious men and women, who will occupy the front ranks about him, to all appearance by chance, and will restrain the ranks the rest out of respect as it will appear for good order. This will sow an example of restraint also in others. If a petitioner appears among the people trying to hand a petition and forcing his way through the ranks, the first ranks must receive the petition and before the eyes of the petitioner pass it to the ruler, so that all may know that what is handed in reaches its destination, that, consequently, there exists a control of the ruler himself. The aureole of power requires for its existence that the people may be able to say: "If the king knew of this," or: "the king will hear of it."

With the establishment of official secret defense the mystical prestige of authority disappears: given a certain audacity, and everyone counts himself master of it, the sedition-monger is conscious of his strength, and when occasion serves watches for the moment to make an attempt upon authority. . . . . For the *goyim* we have been preaching something else, but by that very fact we are enabled to see what measures of overt defense have brought them to. . . . .

Criminals with us will be arrested at the first more or less well-grounded *suspicion;* it cannot be allowed that out of fear of a possible mistake an opportunity should be given of escape to persons suspected of a political lapse or crime, for in these matters we shall be literally merciless. If it is still possible, by stretching a point, to admit a reconsideration of the motive causes in simple crimes, there is no possibility of excuse for persons occupying themselves with questions in which nobody except the government can understand anything..... And it is not all goverments that understand true policy.

PROTOCOL NO. 19

The right of presenting petitions and projects. Sedition. Indictment of political crimes. Advertisement of political crimes.

If we do not permit any independent dabbling in the political we shall on the other hand encourage every kind of report or petition with proposals for the government to examine into all kinds of projects for the amelioration of the condition of the people; this will reveal to us the defects or else the fantasies of our subjects, to which we shall respond either by accomplishing them or by a wise rebutment to prove the short-sightedness of one who judges wrongly.

Sedition-mongering is nothing more than the yapping of a lap-dog at an elephant. For a government well organized, not from the police but from the public point of view, the lap-dog yaps at the elephant in entire unconsciousness of its strength and importance. It needs no more than to take a good example to show the relative importance of both and the lap-dogs will cease to yap and will wag their tails the moment they set eyes on an elephant.

In order to destroy the prestige of heroism for political crime we shall send it for trial in the category of thieving, murder, and every kind of abominable and filthy crime. Public opinion will then confuse in its conception this category of crime with the disgrace attaching to every other and will brand it with the same contempt.

We have done our best, and I hope we have succeeded, to obtain that the *goyim* should not arrive at this means of contending with sedition. It was for this reason that through the Press and in speeches, indirectly — in cleverly compiled schoolbooks on history, we have advertised the martyrdom alleged to have been accepted by sedition-mongers for the idea of the commonweal. This advertisement has increased the contingent of liberals and has brought thousands of *goyim* into the ranks of our live-stock cattle.

PROTOCOL NO. 20

FINANCIAL PROGRAMME. Progressive tax. Stamp progressive taxation. Exchequer, interest-bearing papers and stagnation of currency. Method of accounting. Abolition of ceremonial displays. Stagnation of capital. Currency issue. Gold standard. Standard of cost of working man power. Budget. State loans. One per cent. interest series. Industrial shares. Rulers of the *goyim*: courtiers and favouritism, masonic agents.

To-day we shall touch upon the financial programme, which I put off to the end of my report as being the most difficult, the crowning and the decisive point of our plans. Before entering upon it I will remind you that I have already spoken before by way of a hint when I said that the sum total of our actions is settled by the question of figures.

When we come into our kingdom our autocratic government will avoid, from a principle of self-preservation, sensibly burdening the masses of the people with taxes, remembering that it plays the part of father and protector. But as State organization costs dear it is necessary nevertheless to obtain the funds required for it. It will, therefore, elaborate with particular precaution the question of equilibrium in this matter.

Our rule, in which the king will enjoy the legal fiction that everything in his State belongs to him (which may easily be translated into fact), will be enabled to resort to the lawful confiscation of all sums of every kind for the regulation of their circulation in the State. From this follows that taxation will best be covered by a progressive tax on property. In this manner the dues will be paid without straitening or ruining anybody in the form of a percentage of the amount of property. The rich must be aware that it is their duty to place a part of their superfluities at the disposal of the State since the State guarantees them security of possession of the rest of their property and the right of honest gains, I say honest, for the control over property will do away with robbery on a legal basis.

This social reform must come from above, for the time is ripe for it — it is indispensable as a pledge of peace.

The tax upon the poor man is a seed of revolution and works to the detriment of the state which in hunting after the trifling is missing the big. Quite apart from this, a tax on capitalists diminishes the growth of wealth in private hands in which we have in these days concentrated it as a counterpoise to the government strength of the *goyim* — their State finances.

A tax increasing in a percentage ratio to capital will give a much larger venue than the present individual or property tax, which is useful to us now for the sole reason that it excites trouble and discontent among the *goyim*.

The force upon which our king will rest consist in the equilibrium and the guarantee of peace, for the sake of which things it is indispensable that the capitalists should yield up a portion of their incomes for the sake of the secure working of the machinery of the State. State needs must be paid by those who will not feel the burden and have enough to take from.

Such a measure will destroy the hatred of the poor man for the rich, in whom he will see a necessary financial support for the State, will see in him the organizer of peace and well-being since he will see that it is the rich man who is paying the necessary means to attain these things.

In order that payers of the educated classes should not too much distress themselves over the new payments they will have full accounts given them of the destination of those payments, with the exception of such sums as well be appropriated for the needs of the throne and the administrative institutions.

He who reigns will not have any properties of his own once all in the State represents his patrimony, or else the one would be in contradiction to the other; the fact of holding private means would destroy the right of property in the common possessions of all.

Relatives of him who reigns, his heirs excepted, who will be maintained by the resources of the State, must enter the ranks of servants of the State or must work to obtain the right to property; the privilege of royal blood must not serve for the spoiling of the treasury.

Purchase, receipt of money or inheritance will be subject to the payment of a stamp progressive tax. Any transfer of property, whether money or other, without evidence of payment of this tax which will be strictly registered by names, will render the former holder liable to pay interest on the tax from the moment of transfer of these sums up to the discovery of his evasion of declaration of the transfer. Transfer documents must be presented weekly at the local treasury office with notifications of the name, surname and permanent place of residence of the former and the new holder of the property. This transfer with register of names must begin from a. definite sum which exceeds the ordinary expenses of buying and selling of necessaries, and these will be subject to payment only by a stamp impost of a definite percentage of the unit.

Just strike an estimate of how many times such taxes as these will cover the revenue of the *goyim States*.

The State exchequer will have to maintain a definite complement of reserve sums, and all that is collected above that complement must be returned into circulation. On these sums will be organized public works. The initiative in works of this kind, proceeding from State sources, will bind the working class firmly to the interests of the State and to those who reign. From these same sums also a part will be set aside as rewards of inventiveness and productiveness.

On no account should so much as a single unit above the definite and freely estimated sums be retained in the State treasuries, for money exists to be circulated and any kind of stagnation of money acts ruinously on the running of the State machinery, for which it is the lubricant; a stagnation of the lubricant may stop the regular working of the mechanism.

The substitution of interest-bearing paper for a part of the token of exchange has produced exactly this stagnation. The consequences of this circumstance are already sufficiently noticeable.

A court of account will also be instituted by us and in it the ruler will find at any moment a full accounting for State income and expenditure, with the exception of the curret monthly account, not yet made up, and that of the preceding month, which will not yet have been delivered.

The one and only person who will have no interest in robbing the State is its owner, the ruler. This is why his personal control will remove the possibility of leakages of extravagances.

The representative function of the ruler at receptions for the sake of etiquette, which absorbs so much invaluable time, will be abolished in order that the ruler may have time for control and consideration. His power will not then be split up into fractional parts among time-serving favourites who surround the throne for its pomp and splendour, and are interested only in their own and not in the common interests of the State.

Economic crises have been produced by us from the *goyim* by no other means than the withdrawal of money from circulation. Huge capitals have stagnated, withdrawing money from States, which were constantly obliged to apply to those same stagnant capitals for loans. These loans burdened the finances of the State with the payment of interest and made them the bond slaves of these capitals. . . . The concentration of industry in the hands of capitalists out of the hands of small masters has drained away all the juices of the peoples and with them also of the States. . . .

The present issue of money in general does not correspond with the requirements per head, and cannot therefore satisfy all the needs of the workers. The issue of money ought to correspond with the growth of population and thereby children also must absolutely be reckoned as consumers of currency from the day of their birth. The revision of issue is a material question for the whole world.

You are aware that the gold standard has been the ruin of the States which adopted it, for it has not been able to satisfy the demands for money, the more so that we have removed gold from circulation as far as possible.

With us the standard that must be introduced is the cost of working-man power, whether it be reckoned in paper or in wood. We shall make the issue of money in accordance with the normal requirements of each subject, adding to the quantity with every birth and substracting with every death.

The accounts will be managed by each department (the French administrative division), each circle.

In order that there may be no delays in paying out of money for State needs the sums and terms of such payments will be fixed by decree of the ruler; this will do away with the protection by a ministry of one institution to the detriment of others.

The budgets of income and expenditure will be carried out side by side that they may not be obscured by distance one to another.

The reforms projected by us in the financial institutions and principles of the *goyim* will be clothed by us in such forms as will alarm nobody. We shall point out the necessity of reforms in consequence of the disorderly darkness into which the *goyim* by their irregularities have plunged the finances. The first irregularity, as we shall point out, consists in their beginning with drawing up a single budget which year after year grows owing to the following cause: this budget is dragged out to half the year, then they demand a budget to put things right, and this they expend in three months, after which they ask for a supplementary budget, and all this er ds with a liquidation budget. But, as the budget of the following year is drawn up in accordance with the sum of the total addition, the annual departure from the normal reaches as much as 50 percent in a year, and so the annual budget is trebled in ten years. Thanks to such methods, allowed by the carelessness of the *goy* States, their treasuries are empty. The period of loans supervenes, and that has swallowed up remainders and brought all the *goy* States to bankruptcy.

You understand perfectly that economic arrangements of this kind, which have been suggested to the *goyim* by us, cannot be carried on by us.

Every kind of loan proves infirmity in the State and a want of understanding of the rights of the State. Loans hang like a sword of Damocles over the heads of rulers, who, instead of taking from their subjects by a temporary tax, come begging with oustretched palm of our bankers. Foreign loans are leeches which there is no possibility of removing from the body of the State until they fall off of themselves or the State flings them off. But the *goy* States do not tear them off; they go on in persisting in putting more on to themselves so that they must inevitably perish, drained by voluntary blood-letting.

What also indeed is, in substance, a loan, especially a foreign loan? A loan is — an issue of government bills of exchange containing a percentage obligation commensurate to the sum of the loan capital. If the loan bears a charge of 5 per cent., then in twenty years the State vainly pays away in interest a sum equal to the loan borrowed, in forty years it is paying a double sum, in sixty—treble, and all the while the debt remains an unpaid debt.

From this calculation it is obvious that with any form of taxation per head the State is baling out the last coppers of the poor taxpayers in order to settle accounts with wealthy foreigners, from whom it has borrowed money instead of collecting these coppers for its own needs without the additional interest.

So long as loans were internal the *goyim* only shuffled money from the pockets of the poor to those of the rich, but when we bought up the necessary person in order to transfer loans into the external sphere all the wealth of States flowed into our cash-boxes and all the *goyim* began to pay us the tribute of subjects.

If the superficiality of *goy* kings on their thrones in regard to State affairs and the venality of ministers or the want of understanding of financial matters on the part of other ruling persons have made their countries debtors to our treasuries to amounts quite impossible to pay it has not been accomplished without on our part heavy expenditure of trouble and money.

Stagnation of money will not be allowed by us and therefore there will be no State-interest bearing paper, except a one-per-cent. series, so that there will be no payment of interest to leeches that suck all the strength out of the State. The right to issue interest-bearing paper will be given exclusively to industrial companies who will find no difficulty in paying interest out of profits, whereas the

State does not make interest on borrowed money like these companies, for the State borrows to spend and not to use in operations.

Industrial papers will be bought also by the government which from being as now a payer of tribute by loan operations will be transformed into a lender of money at a profit. This measure will stop the stagnation of money, parasitic profits and idleness, all of which were useful for us among the *goyim* so long as they were independent but are not desirable under our rule.

How clear is the undeveloped power of thought of the purely brute brains of the *goyim*, as expressed in the fact that they have been borrowing from us with payment of interest without ever thinking that all the same these very moneys plus an addition for payment of interest must be got by them from their own State pockets in order to settle up with us. What could have been simpler than to take the money they wanted from their own people?

But it is a proof of the genius of our chosen mind that we have contrived to present the matter of loans to them in such a light that they have even seen in them an advantage for themselves.

Our accounts, which we shall present when the time comes, in the light of centuries of experience gained by experiments made by us on the *goy* States, will be distinguished by clearness and definiteness and will show at a glance to all men the advantage of our innovations. They will put an end to those abuses to which we owe our mastery over the *goyim*, but which cannot be allowed in our kingdom.

We shall so hedge about our system of accounting that neither the ruler nor the most insignificant public servant will be in a position to divert even the smallest sum from its destination without detection or to direct it in another direction except that which will be once fixed in a definite plan of action.

And without a definite plan it is impossible to rule. Marching along an undetermined road and with undetermined resources brings to ruin by the way heroes and demi-gods.

The *goy* rulers, whom we once upon a time advised should be distracted from State occupations by representatives receptions, observances of etiquette, entertainments, were only screens for our rule. The accounts of favourite courtiers who replaced them in the sphere of affairs were drawn up for them by our agents, and every time gave satisfaction to short-sighted minds by promises that in the future economies and improvements were foreseen...... Economies from what? From new taxes? — were questions that might have been but were not asked by those who read our accounts and projects.....

You know to what they have been brought by this carelessness, to what a pitch of financial disorder. they have arrived, notwithstanding the astonishing industry of their peoples.....

PROTOCOL NO. 21

Internal loans. Debit and taxes. Conversions. Bankruptcy. Savings banks and rentes. Abolition of money markets. Regulation of industrial values.

To what I reported to you at the last meeting I shall now add a detailed explanation of internal loans. Of foreign loans I shall say nothing more, because they have fed us with the national moneys of the *goyim*, but for our State there will be no foreigners, that is, nothing external.

We have taken advantage of the venality of administrators and the slackness of rulers to get our moneys twice, thrice and more times over, by lending to the *goy* governments moneys which were not at all needed by the States. Could anyone do the like in regard to us? .... Therefore, I shall only deal with the details of internal loans.

States announce that such a loan is to be concluded and

open subscriptions for their own bills of exchange, that is, for their interest-bearing paper. That they may be within the reach of all the price is determined at from a hundred to a thousand; and a discount is made for the earliest subscribers. Next day by artificial means the price of them goes up, the alleged reason being that everyone is rushing to buy them. In a few days the treasury safes are as they say overflowing and there's more money than they can do with (why then take it?). The subscription, it is alleged, covers many times over the issue total of the loan: in this lies the whole stage effect — look you, they say, what confidence is shown in the government's bills of exchange.

But when the comedy is played out there emerges the fact that a debit and an exceedingly burdensome debit has been created. For the payment of interest it becomes necessary to have resource to new loans, which do not swallow up but only add to the capital debt. And when this credit is exhausted it becomes necessary by new taxes to cover, not the loan, but only the interest on it. These taxes are a debit employed to cover a debit. . . . .

Later comes the time for conversions, but they deminish the payment of interest without covering the debt, and besides they cannot be made without the consent of the lenders; on announcing a conversion a proposal is made to return the money to those who are not willing to convert their paper. If everybody expressed his unwillingness and demanded his money back, the government would be hooked on their own flies and would be found insolvent and unable to pay the proposed sums. By good luck the subjects of the *goy* governments, knowing nothing about financial affairs, have always preferred losses on exchange and diminution of interest to the risk of new investments of their moneys, and have thereby many a time enabled these governments to throw off their shoulders a debit of several millions.

Nowadays, with external loans, these tricks cannot be

played by the *goyim* for they know that we shall demand all our moneys back.

In this way an acknowledged bankruptcy will best prove to the various countries the absence of any means between the interests of the peoples and of those who rule them.

I beg you to concentrate your particular attention upon this point, and upon the following: nowadays all internal loans are consolidated by so-called flying loans, that is, such as have terms of payment more or less near. These debts consist of moneys paid into the savings banks and reserve funds. It left for long at the disposition of a government these funds evaporate in the payment of interest on foreign loans, and are replaced by the deposit of equivalent amount of *rentes*.

And these last it is which patch up all the leaks in the State treasuries of the *goyim*.

When we ascend the throne of the world all these financial and similar shifts, as being not in accord with our interests, will be swept away so as not to leave a trace, as also will be destroyed all money markets, since we shall not allow the prestige of our power to be shaken by fluctuations of prices set upon our values, which we shall announce by law at the price which represents their full worth without any possibility of lowering or raising. (Raising gives the pretext for lowering, which indeed was where we made a beginning in relation to the values of the *goyim*.)

We shall replace the money markets by grandiose government credit institutions, the object of which will be to fix the price of industrial values in accordance with government views. These institutions will be in a position to fling upon the market five hundred millions of industrial paper in one day, or to buy up for the same amount. In this way all industrial undertakings will come into dependence upon us. You may imagine for yourselves what immense power we shall thereby secure for ourselves. . . . . .

PROTOCOL NO. 22

The secret of what is coming. The evil of many centuries
as the foundation of future well-being. The aureole of
power and its mystical worship.

In all that has so far been reported by me to you, I
have endeavoured to depict with care the secret of what is
coming, of what is past, and of what is going on now,
rushing into the flood of the great events coming already
in the near future, the secret of our relations to the *goyim*
and of financial operations. On this subject there remains
still a little for me to add.

*In our hands is the greatest power of our day — gold:
in two days we can procure from our storehouses any
quantity we may please.*

Surely there is no need to seek further proof that our
rule is predestined by God? Surely we shall not fail with
such wealth to prove that all that evil which for so many
centuries we have had to commit has served at the end of
ends the cause of true well-being—the bringing of everything into order? Though it be even by the exercise of
some violence, yet all the same it will be established. We
shall contrive to prove that we are benefactors who have
restored to the rend and mangled earth the true good and
also freedom of the person, and therewith we shall enable
it to be enjoyed in peace and quiet, with proper dignity
of relations, on the condition, of course, of strict observance of the laws established by us. We shall make plain
therewith that freedom does not consist in dissipation and
in the right of unbridled licence any more than the dignity and force of a man do not consist in the right for everyone to promulgate destructive principles in the nature of
freedom of conscience, equality and the like, that freedom
of the person in no wise consists in the right to agitate
oneself and others by abominable speeches before disorderly mobs, and that true freedom consists in the inviola-

bility of the person who honourably and strictly observes all the laws of life in common, that human dignity is wrapped up in consciousness of the rights and also of the absence of rights of each, and not wholly and solely in fantastic imaginings about the subject of one's *ego*.

Our authority will be glorious because it will be all-powerful, will rule and guide, and not muddle along after leaders and orators shrieking themselves hoarse with senseless words which they call great principles and which are nothing else, to speak honestly, but utopian. . . . Our authority will be the crown of order, and in that is included the whole happiness of man. The aureole of this authority will inspire a mystical bowing of the knee before it and a reverent fear before it of all the peoples. True force makes no terms with any right, not even with that of God: none dare come near to it so as to take so much as a span from it away.

PROTOCOL NO. 23

Reduction of the manufacture of articles of luxury. Small master production. Unemployment. Prohibition of drunkenness. Killing out of the old society and its resurrection in a new form. The chosen one of God.

That the peoples may become accustomed to obedience it is necessary to inculcate lessons of humility and therefore to reduce the production of articles of luxury. By this we shall improve morals which have been debased by emulation in the sphere of luxury. We shall re-establish small master production which will mean laying a mine under the private capital of manufacturers. This is indispensable also for the reason that manufacturers on the grand scale often move, though not always consciously, the thoughts of the masses in directions against the government. A people of small masters knows nothing of unemployment and this binds him closely with existing order, and consequently with the firmness of authority. Unemployment is a most perilous thing for a government. For us its part will have been played out the moment authority is transferred into our hands. Drunkenness also will be prohibited by law and punishable as a crime against the humanness of man who is turned into a brute under the influence of alcohol.

Subjects, I repeat once more, give blind obedience only to the strong hand which is absolutely independent of them, for in it they feel the sword for defense and support against social scourges. . . . What do they want with an angelic spirit in a king? What they have to see in him is the personification of force and power.

The supreme lord who will replace all now existing rulers, dragging on their existence among societies demoralized by us, societies that have denied even the authority of God, from whose midst breaks out on all sides the fire of anarchy, must first of all proceed to quench this all-devouring flame. Therefore he will be obliged to kill off those existing societies, though he should drench them with his own blood, that he may resurrect them again in the form of regularly organized troops fighting consciously with every kind of infection that may cover the body of the State with sores.

This Chosen One of God is chosen from above to demolish the senseless forces moved by instinct and not reason, by brutishness and not humanness. These forces now triumph in manifestations of robbery and every kind of violence under the mask of principles of freedom and rights. They have overthrown all forms of social order to erect on the ruins the throne of the King of the Jews; but their part will be played out the moment he enters into his kingdom. Then it will be necessary to sweep them away from his path, on which must be left no knot, no splinter.

Then will it be possible for us to say to the peoples of the world: "Give thanks to God and bow the knee before him who bears on his front the seal of the predestination of man, to which God himself has led his star that none other but Him might free us from all the before-mentioned forces and evils."

PROTOCOL NO. 24

Confirming the roots of King David (?). Training of the king. Setting aside of direct heirs. The king and three of his sponsors. The king is fate. Irreproachability of exterior morality of the King of the Jews.

I pass now to the method of confirming the dynastic roots of King David to the last strata of the earth.

This confirmation will first and foremost be included in that in which to this day has rested the force of conservatism by our learned elders of the conduct of all the affairs of the world, in the directing of the education of thought of all humanity.

Certain members of the seed of David will prepare the kings and their heirs, selecting not by right of heritage but by eminent capacities, inducting them into the most secret mysteries of the political, into schemes of government, but providing always that none may come to knowledge of the secrets. The object of this mode of action is that all may know that government cannot be entrusted to those who have not been inducted into the secret places of its art. . . . .

To these persons only will be taught the practical application of the aforenamed plans by comparison of the experiences of many centuries, all the observations on the politico-economic moves and social sciences — in a word, all the spirit of laws which have been unshakably established by nature herself for the regulation of the relations of humanity.

Direct heirs will often be set aside from ascending the throne if in their time of training they exhibit frivolity, softness and other qualities that are the ruin of authority, which render them incapable of governing and in themselves dangerous for kingly office.

Only those who are unconditionally capable for firm, even if it be to cruelty, direct rule will receive the reins of rule from our learned elders.

In case of falling sick with weakness of will or other form of incapacity, kings must by law hand over the reins of rule to new and capable hands.

The king's plans of action for the current moment, and all the more so for the future, will be unknown, even to those who are called his closest counsellors.

Only the king and the three who stood sponsor for him will know what is coming.

In the person of the king who with unbending will is master of himself and of humanity all wiss discern as it were fate with its mysterious ways. None will know what the king wishes to attain by his dispositions, and therefore none will dare to stand across an unknown path.

It is understood that the brain reservoir of the king must correspond in capacity to the plan of government it has to contain. It is for this reason that he will ascend the throne not otherwise than after examination of his mind by the aforesaid learned elders.

That the people may know and love their king it is indispensable for him to converse in the market-places with his people. This ensures the necessary clinching of the two forces which are now divided one from another by us by the terror.

This terror was indispensable for us till the time comes for both these forces separately to fall under our influence.

The King of the Jews must not be at the mercy of his passions, and especially of sensuality: on no side of his character must he give brute instinct power over his mind. Sensuality worse than all else disorganizes the capacities of the mind and clearness of views, distracting the thoughts to the worst and most brutal side of human activity.

The prop of humanity in the person of the supreme lord of all the world of the holy seed of David must sacrifice to his people all personal inclinations.

Our supreme lord must be of an exemplary irreproachability.

About the Authors

Rabbi Abraham Cooper has been the associate dean of the Simon Wiesenthal Center, since it's founding by Rabbi Marvin Hier in 1977.

A longtime human rights activist on five continents, Cooper's extensive involvement in Soviet Jewry included visiting refuseniks in the 1970s, helping to open the first Jewish Cultural Center in Moscow in the 1980s, lecturing at the Soviet Academy of Sciences in the 1990s, and confronting Pamyat in 2001.

For over a quarter of a century, Rabbi Cooper has overseen the Wiesenthal Center's international social action agenda including worldwide anti-Semitism, Nazi war crimes and restitution, terrorism, and tolerance education. He is widely recognized as a pioneer and international authority on digital hate and the Internet and has testified before the UN, US Senate, Japanese Diet, French Parliament, and Israel's Knesset.

Rabbi Cooper has coordinated international conferences on anti-Semitism at UNESCO headquarters in Paris, on Holocaust Restitution in Geneva, and on Digital Hate in Berlin. Cooper's trailblazing work in Asia has facilitated new venues in intergroup relations in Japan, the People's Republic of China and India. He was a leader of the Center's 1992 China mission that brought the first Jewish-sponsored exhibition to the world's most populous nation.

In 2001, Rabbi Cooper was a delegate at the infamous UN Conference in Durban, South Africa, where he emerged as a leading spokesman in defense of the Jewish people and the State of Israel.

Rabbi Cooper is the editor-in-chief of *Response* magazine, has written a children's book and the World Book Encyclopedia's entry on Raoul Wallenberg and authored exhibitions ranging from Simon Wiesenthal to Jackie Robinson. He also supervised the production of the Interactive Learning Center on the Holocaust (available at www.wiesenthal.com) for the Center's renowned Museum of Tolerance.

Rabbi Cooper has his BA and MS from Yeshiva University and a Ph.D. from the Jewish University of America.

Steven Leonard Jacobs holds the Aaron Aronov Endowed Chair in Judaic Studies at The University of Alabama, Tuscaloosa, AL, where he is also Associate Professor of Religious Studies. His primary research interests are the Holocaust and Genocide and post-Holocaust Biblical re-interpretation. Among his books are *Shirt Bialik: A New and Annotated Translation of Chaim Nachman Bialik's Epic Poems* (1987); *Raphael Lemkin's Thoughts on Nazi Genocide: Not Guilty?* (1992); *Contemporary Christian and Contemporary Jewish Religious Responses to the Shoah* (1993, 2 volumes); *Rethinking Jewish Faith: The Child of a Survivor Responds* (1994); *The Holocaust Now: Contemporary Christian and Jewish Thought* (1996); *Encyclopedia of Genocide* (1999; Associate Editor); *Pioneers of Genocide Studies* (2002; Co-Editor). He is also active in a number of genocide prevention and Holocaust awareness organizations, and serves as the Secretary-Treasurer of the International Association of Genocide Scholars.

Mark Weitzman is the Director of the Task Force against Hate and Terrorism and the Associate Director of Education for the Simon Wiesenthal Center where he is also the chief representative of the Center to the United Nations. Mr. Weitzman is a member of the official US delegation to the Task Force for International Cooperation on Holocaust Education, Remembrance and Research and the Vice-President of the Association of Holocaust Organizations. He is a member of the official Jewish-Catholic Dialogue Group of New York and of the advisory body of the Aegis Trust, as well as the advisory panel of Experts on Freedom of Religion or Belief for the Organization for Security and Co-operation in Europe (OSCE). In June of 1999 Mr. Weitzman was honored with the Distinguished Service Award by the Center of Hate and Extremism at the Richard Stockton College of New Jersey.

As a recognized expert in the fields of extremism and cyberhate he has lectured and worked with various groups ranging from the European Commission, European Union and the U.S. Embassy in Berlin to the U.S. Army and the FBI.

He was on the board of advisors for the *Companion Guide to the film Shoah* (1987) and for *Historical Case Studies: The Holocaust* (1996). His publications include editing and contributing to *Kristallnacht: A Resource Book and Program Guide* (1988), *Dignity and Defiance: Confronting Life and Death in the Warsaw Ghetto* (1993) and *The New Lexicon of Hate* (1998), as well as the annual CD report *Digital Hate and Terrorism* (2000–2003). He has published numerous scholarly articles in the fields of Holocaust, antisemitism and extremism, and is a contributor to the forthcoming *Encyclopedia of Genocide and Crimes Against Humanity*.